Digital Information Culture

Chandos Internet Series

Chandos' new series of books are aimed at all those individuals interested in the internet. They have been specially commissioned to provide the reader with an authoritative view of current thinking. If you would like a full listing of current and forthcoming titles, please visit our web site **www.chandospublishing.com** or contact Hannah Grace-Williams on e-mail info@chandospublishing.com or telephone number +44 (0) 1993 848726.

New authors: we are always pleased to receive ideas for new titles; if you would like to write a book for Chandos, please contact Dr Glyn Jones on e-mail gjones@chandospublishing.com or telephone number +44 (0) 1993 848726.

Bulk orders: some organisations buy a number of copies of our books. If you are interested in doing this, we would be pleased to discuss a discount. Please contact Hannah Grace-Williams on e-mail info@chandospublishing.com or telephone number +44 (0) 1993 848726.

Digital Information Culture: The individual and society in the digital age

Luke Tredinnick

Chandos Publishing
Oxford · England

Chandos Publishing (Oxford) Limited
TBAC Business Centre
Avenue 4
Station Lane
Witney
Oxford OX28 4BN
UK
Tel: +44 (0) 1993 848726 Fax: +44 (0) 1865 884448
E-mail: info@chandospublishing.com
www.chandospublishing.com

First published in Great Britain in 2008

ISBN:
978 1 84334 160 4 (paperback)
978 1 84334 170 3 (hardback)
1 84334 160 3 (paperback)
1 84334 170 0 (hardback)

British Library Cataloguing-in-Publication Data.
A catalogue record for this book is available from the British Library.

Typeset by Domex e-Data Pvt. Ltd.

For Elizabeth

Contents

About the author

Luke Tredinnick is a senior lecturer in information management at London Metropolitan University and course leader for the MSc on digital information management. He specialises in digital information management and the social and cultural impact of computing technology. His other published works include *Why Intranets Fail (and How to Fix Them)*, published by Chandos in 2004, and *Digital Information Contexts*, published by Chandos in 2006.

The author may be contacted at:
l.tredinnick@londonmet.ac.uk

Prologue

This book is intended as a companion to *Digital Information Contexts*, published in 2006. *Digital Information Contexts* sought to critique the existing theoretical assumptions of the information profession, and their appropriateness in the digital age. It also sought to map out new theoretical perspectives that could be applied to the understanding of digital information and digital technology. That earlier book provides most of the methodological and theoretical foundation for this work. As a consequence, except where drawing on aspects of theory unaddressed in that previous work, this book is light on theoretical baggage. Although it is not necessary to have read *Digital Information Contexts* to understand this book, where appropriate endnotes allude to chapters in that work which support the arguments presented here.

This book can be broadly placed within an interpretivist paradigm – which is to say that it treats phenomena as things that are given value and meaning through their interpretation within social contexts, rather than as things that possess objective values and meaning in their own right. This is particularly the case when it addresses aspects of the cultural world, such as texts, artworks, films or audio recordings. It will be argued that the values on which we draw in creating meaning from cultural objects reflect a kind of negotiation between those objects, their context and their audiences. This book can also be placed within a critical tradition: it seeks to *persuade* and not to *demonstrate*. Much of the literature about the impact of digital technology on society and culture tends to root itself in empirical evidence, and often in quantitative evidence to support a conjecture about socio-cultural change. The value of these studies is measured against the real world that they seek to reflect and contain. There is no harm in that approach, but it is not what this book is about. Where it draws on empirical studies they are intended as illustrative rather than demonstrative. Much of the theoretical background for this work belongs in the post-structuralist tradition. But the book also draws on ideas from post-modernism, particularly in its treatment of historical objectivity and the idea of objective truth.

Part I
Culture and technology

1

The meaning of culture

This is a book about the influence of digital information technology on the way we live our lives in the early twenty-first century. To call a book *Digital Information Culture* is to make a tacit assertion: that digital technologies have had, or are having, a transformational effect on cultural values. Such an assertion encloses a set of basic assumptions that are worth detailing. The first of these is that 'culture' furnishes us with the kind of concept that can be subjected to analysis. Culture has been called one of the two or three most complex words in the English language (Williams, 1983: 87). It is also, perhaps, one of the most politicised. This chapter will explore how the idea of culture has developed during the past century and a half, and what this means for the tacit assertion enclosed in the title of this book.

Reflexivity, performativity and culture

In 2001 the UN Educational, Scientific and Cultural Organization defined culture as 'the set of distinctive spiritual, material, intellectual and emotional features of society or a social group, [that] encompasses, in addition to art and literature, lifestyles, ways of living together, value systems, traditions and beliefs' (UNESCO, 2001). While as bland as it is inclusive, this definition emphasises several points that will be touched on in the current chapter. Firstly there is the idea that culture broadly encompasses three elements: social relations within a social system ('lifestyles, ways of living together'); idea systems that mediate social practices and social relations ('value systems, traditions, and beliefs'); and the material products of social and cultural practices ('art and literature'). With the latter of these can perhaps also be included the desire or drive informing their creation, itself suggesting some seemingly essential quality of human aspirations (maybe what Fukuyama (1992) terms *thymos,* or the drive for recognition).[1] Secondly we can note that to be considered aspects of culture, such material products, social relations and idea systems must be 'distinctive', in this case 'of a society or a social group'. Not any old ideas, practices or relations will do, only those that are characteristic of, and perhaps unique to, particular social groupings and their identity.

UNESCO's declaration clearly aspires to define culture in ways both non-contentious and inclusive, but to this end it perhaps unwittingly incorporates tensions central to the development of the idea over the past two centuries. While on the basis of this definition almost anything can be included among the 'spiritual, material, intellectual and emotional features of a society or group', almost nothing seems entirely distinctive enough of any particular society or social group either. When culture counts as almost everything on the one hand, and next to nothing on the other, we find ourselves with a kind of irresolvable tension between that which is significant enough and that which is too significant by far. Also of interest is the way in which the three elements of culture contained by the definition are coordinated within it. 'In addition to art and literature' are these other things, at one and the same time a kind of addendum to the statement yet also central to it, afforded more emphasis by being outlined in greater detail. Literature and art may be the starting point of the definition, but they are not its particular focus, describing what is least contentious about the idea of culture to be mentioned in passing only as a means of establishing a more comprehensive, inclusive and perhaps democratic overview. Once the given aspects of culture are dispatched, the definition can move to throw light on its more intangible components.

And who could begrudge UNESCO its apparent coyness? Art and literature imply an old-fashioned idea of culture as the sum total of human intellectual and aesthetic attainment, an idea that we would possibly rather leave behind. But this reluctance to confront the tacit valorisation of certain privileged forms and traditions conceals a sleight of hand. These two material aspects of culture – literature and art, and everything that is implied by them – are only two kinds of cultural product among many, but nevertheless the only two that have been furnished with a particular status through their explicit inclusion, even if only in passing. They are the nucleus of the definition into which other aspects of culture can be incorporated only 'in addition'. This suggests a number of questions: why literature and art, and not other tangible aspects of culture, such as film, television, architecture and digital computing? Why their special status in the sentence, their conspicuous isolation in a subordinate clause? What is literary about literature and artistic about art, anyway? Is *The Origin of Species* also literature and the Acropolis also art, and if we accept them to be so, is their real cultural value as literature and art rather than as science and architecture? Or do we otherwise have to find a place for these things elsewhere in the definition? This crucible of culture into which we can pour things 'in addition to art and literature' seems established on the idea that these two privileged forms are themselves a kind of catalyst, the seeds out of which social relationships and idea systems are grown, or perhaps a dominant cultural mode through which these other and additional things are mediated.

The manner in which UNESCO's definition unravels reflects the tricky nature of the concept it is seeking to contain. Enclosed by it are tensions that reflect both the history of our understanding of culture and its political bite. Eagleton (2000: 1) has commented that culture 'charts within its semantic unfolding humanity's own historic shift from rural to urban existence, pig-farming to Picasso, tilling the soil to splitting the atom'. The very idea of culture reminds us of the rapid changes in social life through the industrial and post-industrial periods. And this brings us to a further point about our preoccupation with culture emphasised by UNESCO's declaration: that whatever the merits of any particular definition, the attempt to articulate an understanding of culture is most importantly an assertion of the centrality of the concept to the way in which we understand ourselves and our social situation. The declaration functions as a kind of *performative* gesture, asserting a particular idea of culture not only through what it says, but also through the act of stating it.[2] How we understand culture is also a measure of our cultural values; it encloses a reflexive anxiety about our own ways of life, traditions and beliefs – a point which will be raised again towards the end of this chapter. Not just culture, then, but also the very idea of culture saturates our whole sense of self.

This perhaps goes partway to explaining why culture has become such a preoccupation of the modern age; because the importance of the idea of culture during the past century and a half is difficult to deny. It is, furthermore, something that we should want to explain if we are to understand the changes of the digital age. To do so, we need to explore how culture developed its peculiarly reflexive action. This chapter will trace the emergence of different ideas of culture through the industrial and post-industrial period. It does not pretend to present an exhaustive overview of a word that has had more written about it than almost any other,[3] but it will draw out some themes of particular interest to this book.

Aspects of culture

The modern connotations of *culture* have, in T.S. Eliot's words, 'not a long history' (1948: 21). Deriving from the Latin word *colere,* it originally described the tending of natural growth in husbandry and agriculture (Eagleton, 2000). By the sixteenth century its meaning had been extended to human development, resulting in the habituation of the term in its application to humans and its increased abstraction towards general, rather than particular, processes of growth (Williams, 1983). But although used in something similar to its modern sense in prior ages, borrowing its metaphorical bite from the jaws of nature put under till and plough, it was in response to the industrial revolution that culture developed its peculiarly reflexive action.

The work most associated with this change was Matthew Arnold's *Culture and Anarchy.* Culture became for Arnold a means of confronting industrialisation's dehumanising effects. In part this concerned the social consequences of industrial machinery; Arnold (1869: 54) attacked the 'idolatry of machinery' and complained that 'faith in machinery [...] is our besetting danger' (ibid.: 16). But the work also reflects an anxiety at the pace and extent of social change following in industrialisation's wake, identified with the growth of a 'strong individualism' antithetical to 'the idea of perfection as an harmonious expansion of human nature' (ibid.: 15). Arnold stressed culture's relationship with the refinement of particular traditions centred on a limited ranged of social practices, institutions and forms. Culture became 'a pursuit of our total perfection by means of getting to know [...] the best which has been thought and said in the world' (ibid.: vii). This definition encloses two elements: the rarefied products of the intellectual tradition set in opposition to the products of industrialisation and mass publishing; and a coming to knowledge of that tradition through reflection, criticism and discrimination. Culture was not for Arnold merely a collection of privileged cultural forms, but a particular relationship with the past drawing on 'all the voices of human experience that have been heard' (ibid.: 13). It played an active part in lived experience; 'not a having and a resting, but a growing and a becoming' (ibid.: 13) developed through 'disinterested and active use of reading, reflection and observation' (ibid.: 221). With its pursuit therefore also came a moral imperative: the desire to make the best of the intellectual tradition prevail, through which its 'moral, social, and beneficent character [...] becomes manifest' (ibid.: 12).

Arnold's critique inaugurated a discourse that spanned almost a century, drawing under its wing some of the leading names of pre-war cultural criticism. To the writers who made up this eclectic group, the electronic media and communications technologies of the early twentieth century heralded an inexorable decline in values. The literary critic F.R. Leavis epitomises the caustic tone of much of this analysis. He defined culture as the use of 'the language, the changing idiom, upon which fine living depends' (Leavis, [1930] 2006: 13). Lamenting the 'so much more desperate plight of culture today' (ibid.: 13), Leavis argued that '"civilisation" and "culture" are coming to be antithetical terms' (ibid.: 18). Industry, mass publishing and mass communications had initiated 'change in habit and the circumstances of life at a rate for which we have no parallel' and threatened that 'what has been lost may be irrecoverable or forgotten' (ibid.: 13). Leavis struck a fatalistic note, writing 'it is in vain to resist the triumph of the machine' (ibid.: 17), and dismissing mass culture as a woeful 'levelling down' (ibid.: 14, 18). Where Arnold had invested faith in educational reform, Leavis saw only the futility of a continued erosion of cultural values. As it emerged into the twentieth century, the idea of culture became if anything more exclusive, refined and unforgiving.

It does not need underlining that the idea of culture as an eternal pursuit of moral and intellectual perfection placed under threat by the material realities of the industrialised economy represents in Williams's (1981: 11) terms 'a confidently partial dimension of reference'. At its heart is an unforgiving élitism reflecting the outlook of a particular social class and tending to privilege certain cultural forms and intellectual ideals at the expense of the wider social experience. This élitism is tacit in the unarticulated values that inform the distinction between different cultural forms. Arnold (1869: 258) described those values as merely 'right reason' and the 'ability to see things as they really are'. Writing later, Leavis (1952) more explicitly refused to elaborate on the critical values underpinning his work. By remaining unarticulated, those values disarm dissent by claiming for themselves the status of common sense; right reason is what remains when the prejudices of mass civilisation are stripped away.

However, there is perhaps more value in recognising the historical context within which this paroxysm of anxiety was formed than there is in outlining precisely the kinds of experience that it marginalised. This partial idea of culture was developed in the face of unprecedented social transformation: the growth of scientific knowledge, the transformation of the cities, the rise of the working classes, the expansion of education and literacy, the growth of mass publishing and later the mechanisation of war and the emergence of mass media. It contained not only the anxiety created by that rapid social change, but also its own mourning for an apparently declining way of life. Eagleton (2000: 11) has described this as ‘a full blown quarrel between tradition and modernity’. But if this is the case, then it is also a quarrel between different versions of tradition. Under their guidance, the idea of tradition was transformed into a narrative of intellectual betterment. But while providing a driving force for intellectual emancipation, this idea also concealed its own dependency on the very changes it attacked. The critical circles to which the writers in the culture and civilisation tradition belonged were rooted in the eighteenth- and nineteenth-century literary periodicals (Eagleton, 1984), themselves a part of the expansion of publishing, and the rise of leisure. The idea of culture they valorised belonged to the same printing press that threatened to destroy it. Their critique of culture therefore ultimately eroded its own foundations, but in the process it exemplified how the idea of culture could become both the object of criticism and the very site of a struggle over identity.

If the critique of the culture and civilisation tradition is undermined by its retreat into an uneasy idealism, then out of the European Marxist tradition emerged a view of culture that was rooted in the conditions of the material world. The influence of Karl Marx on the discourse of culture has been significant. In part this is due to an apparently culture-shaped hole in his economic theory. Marx’s distinction between the economic base and its expression in the socio-political superstructure implied that culture was anchored in the material conditions of its production, but precisely how remained unclear. Although a component in his thinking from an early stage, his most famous articulation of this model was published in 1859:

> In the social production of their life, men enter into definite relations that are indispensable and independent of their will, relations of production which correspond to a definite stage of development of their material productive forces. The sum total of these relations of production constitutes the economic structure of society, the real foundation, on which rises a legal and political superstructure and to which correspond definite forms of social consciousness. The mode of production of material life conditions the social, political and intellectual life process in general. It is not the consciousness of men that determines their being, but, on the contrary, their social being that determines their consciousness. (Marx, [1859] 1968: 181)

The significance of this passage for the idea of culture turns on the interpretation of *determines*. One reading understands the economic base to be the single determining factor in the shape of not only the socio-cultural superstructure, but also its constituent parts. This results in what Storey (1997: 102) has called 'a vulgar Marxist "reflection theory" of culture, in which the politics of a text or practice are read off from or reduced to the economic conditions of its production'. However, after the death of Marx, Engels ([1890] 2006) argued that to reduce the material and economic base to the single determining factor was to transform the basic proposition 'into a meaningless, abstract, absurd phrase'. He stressed the interplay of a complex of forces that individually 'exercise their influence upon the course of the historical struggles and in many cases predominate in determining their form'. The precise relationship between base and superstructure was both complex and irresolvable, but another Marxist idea offered a means of knitting them together. Almost as rich in meaning as culture itself, ideology usually describes a formal system of real or illusory ideas and beliefs characteristic of a particular class or group (cf. Larrain, 1979). It promised to span the gulf between base and superstructure by describing the tendency for the material interest of particular groups to become projected on to the entire socio-political system.

This general Marxist framework glowers behind one of the more dystopian critiques of culture in a newly technological age. Haunted by both the rise of fascism in Europe and the emerging mass media of the USA, the Frankfurt School developed a bleak analysis of the state of society. Two of the most important writers in this tradition, Max Horkheimer and Theodor Adorno ([1944] 2006: 41), believed technologies of mass media inflicted everything with sameness: 'every branch of culture is unanimous within itself and all are unanimous together'. The industry of culture created a demand for cinema, popular magazines and popular music, but by manipulating aspirations into false desires that it subsequently failed to fulfil, it endlessly cheated consumers of its promises. In the face of capitalist interests, the individual was hopelessly and irrevocably subjugated by the technologies of mass culture; the audiences of new cultural forms had little scope to dissent against, interpret or refine the ideological messages by which they were controlled. Capitalism imposed a rigid social sorting of the subject within the ideological and technological superstructure; Horkheimer and Adorno (ibid.: 50) wrote that 'capitalist production hems them in so tightly, in body and soul, that they unresistingly succumb to whatever is proffered to them [...] they insist unwaveringly on the ideology by which they are enslaved'. While writing from a Marxist perspective, this was Marxism in the face of a political failure.

By addressing both the aesthetic of cultural products and the means of their production, the work of the Frankfurt School in many ways represented an advance on the culture and civilisation tradition. Yet despite this it settled on some disarmingly familiar themes. Horkheimer and Adorno's account of culture was also haunted by the spectre of decline, not into anarchy but into an automata-like subservience to capital and capitalist interests. It also turned on the consequences of mechanisation; aspects of culture 'sing the praises of technical progress' (ibid.: 41) and herald the 'universal victory of the rhythm of mechanical production and reproduction' (ibid.: 50). They shared the culture and civilisation tradition's distaste for the products of mass culture and the explicit élitism emerging in the valorisation of certain cultural forms. Still lacking from the analysis of culture was any recognition of the richness of ordinary lives, the vibrancy of cultural forms produced and consumed within ordinary social practices and their importance to the people who create and consume them.

The second half of the twentieth century brought a significant pluralising of what was allowed the name of culture, reflecting both the changing post-war social situation and the adoption of anthropological and sociological outlooks. During the 1950s and 1960s the anthropologist Claude Lévi-Strauss (1966, 1968) explored the symbolic systems underpinning the exchange of meanings in various cultural forms, practices and traditions, including myths and kinship. Culture became for him a shared system of meanings that shaped the way in which people make sense of the world within a social context; aspects of culture became texts to be decoded. During the 1950s the French structuralist Roland Barthes drew on the work of Lévi-Strauss, publishing *Mythologies* ([1957] 1972), which explored the symbolic codes in everyday cultural artefacts and practices such as wrestling, soap powders and striptease. Within this semiotic tradition, culture became a system of meanings that overlie social practices.

The emerging recognition of the everyday nature of culture is apparent in the work of T.S. Eliot, who, while sharing most of the assumptions of the culture and civilisation tradition, allowed the idea a greater resonance. Eliot was responsible for one of the most elegiac descriptions of culture:

> The reader must remind himself as the author has constantly to do, of how much is here embraced by the term *culture*. It includes all

> the characteristic activities and interests of a people: Derby Day, Henley Regatta, Cowes, the twelfth of August, a cup final, the dog races, the pin table, the dart board, Wensleydale cheese, boiled cabbage cut into sections, beetroot in vinegar, nineteenth-century Gothic churches and the music of Elgar. (Eliot, 1948: 31)

This idea of culture was no longer limited to the best that has been thought and said, but widened to include the kinds of everyday social practices that contribute to social identity: the characteristic aspects of the concrete social practices that define a particular group of people. While romanticising social practices and giving only a nod to working-class life, it was a nod that nevertheless acknowledged the changing post-war social situation. This celebration of the very ordinariness of social lives did not replace the sharper criticism of Arnold and Leavis; indeed, Eliot's highly partial view of culture remains explicit in what he excluded from his list, most notably technologies of mass communications and their products. He continued to project a nostalgic and transitory view of culture rooted in a semi-pastoral and parochial past. Eliot's recognition of a greater plurality of culture was perhaps more a surrender to the changing social situation than a celebration of it, and a surrender to the waning influence of a cultural élite rather than an abandonment of those élitist ideals. He maintained that 'we can distinguish between higher and lower cultures; we can distinguish between advance and regression' (ibid.: 18–19) and asserted that 'our own period is one of decline' (ibid.: 19). However, by developing 'a general or anthropological sense of the word culture' (ibid.: 22), Eliot highlighted just how much of human experience had been previously marginalised. Culture became simply 'a way of life' (ibid.: 41).

This new accommodation of different social outlooks suited post-war Britain, where Marxism had retained an intellectual allure that never quite realised itself in concrete political action, and where an egalitarian mood was filtering through the changed social situation (Turner, 1990). No longer merely the vulgarising of a refined ideal, the products and practices of mass culture became indicative of particular ways of life worthy of study in their own right, and tied to the material conditions in which they were created and consumed. In 1957 the sociologist and literary critic Richard Hoggart published *The Uses of Literacy,* contrasting his experiences growing up in a working-class family in the inter-war years with working-class life on the brink of the social revolution of the 1960s.[4] Hoggart analysed the forms, practices and traditions of working-class life, from the use of libraries, pubs and social clubs to new manifestations of youth culture in the form of milkbars, jukeboxes and pulp magazines. He stressed the organic whole of working-class culture, and the interconnectedness of forms, institutions and traditions. But Hoggart also saw a threat to this diversity and richness posed by increased commercialisation. The new cultural forms of the post-war years displaced without adequately substituting themselves for a culture rooted in the social conditions of those who both consume and produce it (Turner, 1990). As with Eliot, the pluralising of culture gave way to echoes of the culture and civilisation tradition's élitism.

The most important writer in this period was undoubtedly Raymond Williams. Although not the first to take culture as his theme, through a series of works he subjected the idea to a detailed and far-reaching critical analysis. *Culture and Society* (1958) analysed the changing meaning of the word through the industrial and post-industrial periods, exposing its ongoing politicisation. *The Long Revolution* (1961) extended this work, applying the analysis of culture to the contemporary age. His work on culture continued throughout his career, with books like *Television* (1974), *Marxism and Literature* (1977), *Culture* (1981) and *Keywords* (1983) condensing and consolidating his critique. Williams (1977: 108) observed that the Gramscian concept of hegemony both contained and transcended two earlier concepts: culture as a whole social process, and ideology as a system of meanings and values pertaining to a particular class interest. Hegemony became for him the mechanism by which dominant, oppositional and residual values competed through the cycle of emergence and incorporation. But while drawing freely on Marxist theory, Williams remained wary of its distillation of lived experience into rigid ideological formations that tended both to create a social sorting of the subject and to marginalise individual experience. He maintained a view of culture as a 'whole way of life' (Williams, 1961: 63), but unlike Eliot remained ecumenical about the value of different cultural formations and expressions. Culture was the lived 'social experiences in solution' (Williams, 1977: 133) reflecting 'meanings and values as they are actively lived and felt' (ibid.: 132). It was contained within 'structures of feeling', a vaguely defined idea that nevertheless captures the essence of a distillation of the entire social experience into individuals in their lived social being.

This sense of culture was too diffuse for one of Williams's more vocal critics. A historian in the Marxist tradition, E.P. Thompson's major contribution to the culture debate came from his analysis of the development of working-class identity through the industrial period in *The Making of the English Working Class* (1963). Thompson recognised with Williams that the concept of culture could not be separated from the material conditions of cultural production in the way the culture and civilisation tradition had implied, but argued that 'any theory of culture must include the concept of the dialectical interaction between culture and something that is *not* culture', and 'it is the active process – which is at the same time the process through which men make their history – that I am insisting upon' (Thompson, 1961a: 38). By viewing culture as 'a whole way of life', Williams had excised anything to which it could be contrasted. Seeing culture to be less a state of attainment and more a matter of degrees of rarefaction of the material conditions of cultural production, Thompson argued that at one pole was 'the raw material of life experience' and at the other 'all the infinitely complex human disciplines and systems, articulate and inarticulate, formalised in institutions or dispersed in the least formal ways, which "handle", transmit or distort this raw material' (ibid.: 33). He rejected the traditional metaphor of base and superstructure and, subverting Williams's definition, argued instead that culture should be understood as 'the study of relationships between elements in a whole way of *conflict*' (ibid.). Williams's attempt to analyse the idea of culture ultimately merely emphasised how irresolvable that idea remained.[5]

Thompson, Williams and Hoggart became important influences on the foundation of a British cultural studies tradition, and with the establishment of the Birmingham Centre for Contemporary Cultural Studies in 1964, that tradition found its spiritual home. Hoggart became its first director, but while the centre was initially intended to explore lived cultures of different social groups in the mould of *The Uses of Literacy*, it quickly became dominated by research into mass media (Turner, 1990). When Stuart Hall replaced Hoggart in 1968 he brought with him a new theoretical rigour. Hall sought to distance the centre from two previous paradigms that either associated culture with 'the sum of the available descriptions through which societies make sense of and reflect their common experiences', or emphasised 'that aspect of "culture" which refers to social practices' (Hall, [1980] 1986). He instead stressed the relationship between media products and ideology in the signifying systems of cultural texts, drawing on the European semiotic tradition. In 'Encoding/decoding' Hall ([1980] 2006) emphasised the ideological saturation of media texts arising from the conditions of their production, but also acknowledged that their meaning was in part created in their consumption. Individual texts were open to reinterpretation, leading to three different kinds of readings that responded to the ideological basis of media: preferred, oppositional and negotiated.

By concentrating on the products and practices of mass media and popular culture, British cultural studies' idea of culture was in many ways as partial as those it explicitly rejected. It is sometimes commented that in the process cultural studies became an over-theorised discourse, perhaps reflecting both the birth pangs of a new discipline and a tacit insecurity about the critical validity of the forms, practices and traditions it addressed. Notable in this context is the continued dominance of Marxist perspectives within the discourse of culture. There is perhaps a sense in which the study of culture *needs* Marxism to a degree that other critical disciplines do not. Marxism provided an extrinsic validation of the critical significance of the products of mass media and popular culture, tying them to structures of ideology, hegemony, the construction of meaning and social organisation. Those products become not merely particular cultural expressions, but the distillation of broader social structures, power and play that become the tacit objects of interrogation. But at the same time, Marxism denies the products of mass media and popular culture the intrinsic validity reserved for privileged cultural forms such as literature and art, which continue to be encountered on their own terms.

In the early twenty-first century, with the emergence of new critical perspectives that each in their own way work to overcome the heritage of Marxism, the idea of culture is perhaps more complex than it has ever been. Post-modernism, with its shattering of metanarratives and rescuing of marginalised perspectives, has led to not only the idea that culture is in an important sense anything and everything that we define it to be, but also that our experience of culture has splintered into innumerable irreconcilable fragments that undermine shared value systems. Lyotard (1984) described the 'incredulity toward metanarratives' that characterises the post-industrial age: the decline of shared meaning systems, and the cynicism towards truth claims. Baudrillard (1994) described the 'precession of simulacra' that results from mass-communications technology, in which the symbols of culture become mere placeholders, losing their intrinsic meaning and value. Fukuyama (1989, 1992) has implied that with the political domination of the USA, cultural differences lose their meaning. Fredric Jameson (1991) highlighted the commodification of the cultural sphere by late capitalism, and its undermining of shared meaning systems. This attack on the basis of cultural values has led to reconsiderations of previously marginalised cultural forms, perspectives and practices, from post-colonialism to queer theory, and new areas of cultural critique, from an increasing interest in the human body to cybernetics and the post-human.[6]

Complexity theory has taken the critique of culture in a different direction, situating culture as an affect of the social system. Rather than a coherent and unified movement, complexity theory is a term that embraces a heterogeneous collection of ideas that Thrift (1999: 34) describes as an 'economy of concepts'. It is founded on the recognition that some qualities of systems are 'not analytically traceable from the attributes of internal components' (Manson, 2001: 410). These qualities arise not from the aggregated behaviour of individual agents but from their rich interaction. Thrift (1999) writes that 'the chief impulse behind complexity theory is an anti-reductionist one', and complexity has often been set in opposition to reductionism. Urry (2005: 5) writes that 'It is not that the sum is greater than the size of its parts – but that there are system effects that are different from the parts'; in Anderson's (1972) more pithy terms, 'more is different'. To describe culture as an affect of the socio-cultural system is to suggest that it is an emergent quality of a richly interlinked, dynamic, complex system that is built out of the interaction of individuals. This is in turn to say a number of things about it: firstly that it arises out of the rich, dynamic and non-linear interaction of many independent agents; secondly that it emerges as a global effect of many local interactions; and thirdly that it emerges from a system about which in principle we lack perfect information.[7]

Often linked with complexity, meme theory has emerged as another way of explaining culture, describing the propagation of culture through the replication of memes. Richard Dawkins (1976) defined the meme as a 'unit of culture', giving examples of catch-phrases, beliefs, clothes, fashion and music. Like genes, memes use human bodies as vehicles for their self-replication, and are therefore objectively independent of human cognition and human social processes. Balkin (1998: 31) tried to tie meme theory back to the more traditional concept of ideology by developing the idea of cultural software, or the 'collectively created tools that constitute us as persons and that we use to make new tools for understanding the world around us'. Blackmore (1999) argued that the design of our minds can be understood solely through the memetic selection, distinguishing between two types of cultural propagation through replication: copying the cultural product, and copying the instructions for recreating the cultural product. While it is unclear if meme theory constitutes anything more than an analogy between the propagation of genes and ideas, it represents an interesting if underdeveloped field.

Culture and the mythopoeic

With the emergence of these new theories, the idea of culture has become if anything more distant, more abstract and less certain than ever before. But we can begin to say something about the meaning of culture in digital information contexts. Raymond Williams (1983) identified three broad meanings of the term:

- culture as the general process of intellectual, spiritual and aesthetic development;
- culture as a particular way of life, of either a people, a period, a group or humanity in general;
- culture as the works and practices of intellectual and artistic activity.

These three senses of culture broadly map on to those in UNESCO's declaration: social relations within a social system ('lifestyles, ways of living together'); idea systems that mediate social practices and social relations ('value systems, traditions, and beliefs'); and the material products of social and cultural practices ('art and literature'). Some consensus therefore exists over culture's relationship to values, traditions, beliefs, ways of life and the material products of creative or intellectual activity, although within this there is also considerable disagreement. Over time there has been a gradual widening of the idea of culture, a movement from what Williams (1981: 11) terms a 'confidently partial' to a 'significantly total' dimension of reference. This has resulted in the aggregation of meanings within the one concept, rather than a replacement of older ideas with newer. All the many senses of the idea of culture remain alive and vivacious in every use of the word.

In addition we can note that the site of culture extends across every level of society, from the individual to the nation-state and beyond, and across different social formations and groupings, from the family to the workplace. Each level of culture seems complicit with every other: culture's social dimension contains, defines and extends its personal dimension, and vice versa. Culture in digital information contexts does not just imply the shared characteristics and behaviour of bloggers, gamers and participants in *Second Life*, who each perhaps construct their identity with reference to digital technologies. It is also a matter of the general change digital technologies have brought to our lives, self-identity and experiences online and offline. We can also note that culture overlaps and contains other significant concepts in theory: ideology, hegemony, discourse, political economy, tradition, identity, signification, the pastoral and so on. Culture both contains and extends these many different manifestations of social life and social experience. Culture has become the site of the production of meaning and the distillation of experience.

Yet despite these things we are able to say, there remains something profoundly unsettling about a word as chimerical as 'culture' – a discomfiture produced by an idea that has become politicised, heterogeneous and always under constant reconstruction. Something about the idea of culture resists articulation and final definition. It is just beyond our grasp, never quite what we insist it to be, present through its absence. This irreducible complexity of culture permeates the discourse. Eliot (1948: 41) observed that an understanding of culture 'can never be complete: either it is abstract – and the essence escapes – or else it is *lived*'. Engels ([1890] 2006) described the 'innumerable crisscrossing forces, an infinite series of parallelograms of forces which give rise to one resultant – the historical event'. Williams (1977: 133) describes culture as 'social experiences in solution', and as the complex of relationships between elements in 'a whole way of life' (Williams, 1961: 63). Thompson (1961a: 33) stressed 'all the infinitely complex human disciplines and systems, articulate and inarticulate, formalised in institutions or dispersed in the least formal ways'. Stuart Hall has called culture 'a site of convergent interests, rather than a logically or conceptually clarified idea' and observed that 'this "richness" is an area of continuing tension' (Hall, [1980] 1986: 35). For Eagleton (2000: 32) culture is an idea which has become 'both too broad and too narrow to be greatly useful'. But while the idea of culture slips through the gaps of critical discourses like water through our fingers, even to talk of culture is to seek to contain it.

It is notable that this reflexive complexity in the idea of culture emerged at a time when other kinds of shared value and meaning systems were threatened by the encroachment of science and technology. The combined effects of industrialisation, urbanisation and scientific advancement shook the value systems of the late nineteenth century to their core. The idea of culture moved into the vacuum they created, testifying to the anxieties produced by social structures subject to more rapid and comprehensive change under the conditions of technological advancement than at any other time in history. The idea of culture became perhaps a way of clinging on to a sense of continuity in the face of rapid social transformation, of insisting on the importance of our ways of living in the face of their material change, of erecting new shared systems of meaning and of enacting a self-conscious warding-off of the dread of mourning for our forgotten pasts.

This highlights a mythopoeic function of the idea of culture; its implication in mythical formulations that give meaning to our social experiences. By holding the fragmentary nature of the social situation in one encompassing idea, culture allows us to weave stories that explain and give meaning to our social situation. By remaining beyond final articulation and always subject to reinterpretation, culture provides a mechanism for assimilating diverse aspects of experience without reconciling their contradictions, an empty vessel into which to pour disparate ideas, values, anxieties and struggles. It becomes a lens to our social situation, distilling and refracting our experiences of industrialisation, urbanisation, fascism, capitalism, diasporas and other kinds of social change. Through its different guises culture records and testifies to the anxieties of different peoples in different ages. It shapes itself to different narratives of social and cultural change, concealing tacit assumptions and values but generously adapting to new ways of life. And it extends the discourses within which it is deployed, implying both shared values and shared meaning systems that resist analysis and reach out beyond the page to stories of social change. Culture is mythopoeic because it ties us into narratives that give our fleeting experiences substantiality, narratives constructed not out of scientific truths, but out of inexpressible, irresolvable but also irrepressible shared values. Which is why, perhaps, culture is always in opposition to something, whether nature, society, civilisation, science, industry, capital or technology.

And this is ironically to say something quite precise about the idea of culture: that it never represents on any scale (either within nation-states or within families, for example) a unified and stable set of values, belief systems, practices, material products and whatever else, but always represents a disparate and mutable set of such things that together have no essential or common characteristics *until we define them as such*, and which are therefore always under constant construction, always lacking complete and final definition and always subject to reinterpretation. Culture is not an idea, but an ongoing discourse about the nature of our social lives as social beings. This book therefore leaves 'culture' undefined beyond the comments already made; not so much still inchoate as over-determined. And it does so for two reasons: to recognise that the complexity of culture is essential to its nature, and to recognise that to settle on one idea of culture is to reduce it to the concrete and the specific, which is in turn tacitly to valorise particular forms, values and traditions.

Notes

1. A more detailed account of Fukuyama's ideas is contained in Tredinnick (2006), Chapter 8.
2. See Austin (1976) for the idea of performativity.
3. Surveys of the uses of culture include Eagleton (2000); Williams (1958, 1961, 1981, 1983); Kroeber and Kluckhohn (1952).
4. See also Hoggart (1991).
5. See also Thompson (1961b). For discussion of Thompson's critique of Williams's *The Long Revolution*, see Hall ([1980] 1986).
6. See also Tredinnick (2006), Chapter 8.
7. See also Lewin (1999); Waldrop (1992); Johnson (2001); Tredinnick (2006), Chapter 9.

2

Representations of technology

The title of this book contains a tacit assertion about the transformational effects of technology on cultural values, practices, traditions and beliefs: the idea of a *digital information culture* implies some significant difference between our own age and what has come before; a difference contained in, and determined by, our use of technology. The effect of technological change on culture is a question central to many debates about the place of technology in the modern age. The previous chapter traced some of this tension, from Arnold's mistrust of industrial machinery to post-modernism's preoccupation with digital information processing. Over the past century and a half culture and technology have become locked in an ongoing dialogue of optimism and regret. This chapter will explore that relationship in more detail. In particular it will examine the way in which different representations of technology influence our experience and understanding of technology's agency over the cultural world.

Change in the digital age

That a certain kind of transformation to social practices and cultural values has accompanied the rapid adoption of computing technology is on one level difficult to deny. The murmur of information has become an ever-present background noise in our lives; information 'gently but relentlessly drizzles down on us in an invisible, impalpable electric rain' (von Baeyer, 2003: 3). In the digital age radio waves spill out across the air, the ubiquitous network knits together cities and fibre-optic cables are strewn across the ocean beds. When we use loyalty cards our shopping habits are recorded and analysed. When we enter our workplaces and study spaces, smartcards betray our presence. Our social relationships are mediated via e-mail, SMS and the web. Digital cash is replacing coins and notes. Our journeys are guided by satellite, and on the threshold of central London cameras capture the number-plates of every car entering and leaving. It is estimated that the residents of major cities are filmed by CCTV hundreds of times every day (Wood, 2006). When we turn on the television, images from the other side of the globe are juxtaposed with home videos and viewer comments. Our friends in other continents have become more closely integrated into our lives than our next-door neighbours. It may still be just about possible to escape the digital world, but it is becoming increasingly difficult to do so every day.

Yet no matter how apparent the transformation to culture in the wake of the digital revolution, it is a different matter to determine its nature, kind and extent. Some theorists have identified a sea-change in society and culture, a radical break with the past exemplified in theories such as future shock (Toffler, 1970), the global village (McLuhan, 1962, 1964), the post-industrial society (Bell, 1974), the post-modern condition (Lyotard, 1984), the end of history (Fukuyama, 1989, 1992), the network society (Castells, 2000), the death of distance (Cairncross, 1997), the moment of complexity (Taylor, 2001) and the cult of the amateur (Keen, 2007). We are not lost for ways of containing the experience of technological change. The emergence of these disparate ideas, which all in different ways address the meeting point of technology and culture, testifies to the widespread perception that our society is significantly altered in the digital age, and the lives we lead are different from those we used to live. The persistent iteration of the transformational effects of technology on culture plays to the theme of this book, but we should not imagine that it reflects an objective reality of socio-cultural change: it is more complex than that. How we experience the socio-cultural effects of digital technology and how we describe those experiences are enmeshed and entangled.

One question dominates the discourse of technology and culture: does technology determine culture, or do cultural values determine the kinds of technology that come to be developed? On the one hand, by providing some of the material conditions under which culture develops technology seems to intervene in its shape and character. But on the other, technological innovation responds to human desires, needs, aspirations and traditions, and is perhaps therefore a consequence rather than a cause of socio-cultural change. Questions of this kind saturate our experiences in digital contexts: do we immerse ourselves in massively multiplayer role-playing games because technology has changed the way in which we interact, or did the technology of massively multiplayer role-playing games develop because we desired to interact in new ways? Have avatars changed our self-identity, or are they merely the digital realisation of our analogue selves? Does e-mail change, or simply express, our desire to communicate with one another? Do people blog just because they can, or do blogs exist because we felt a need for them; and even if the latter, has that need been transformed in its fulfilment? Are we ultimately in command of the machine, or is the machine in command of us? While questions of this kind tend to imply a false opposition of technology and culture addressed by insisting on the *interplay* of the two, this solution merely obscures rather than explains the nature of that relationship.

To resolve this problem we might choose to distinguish between the *expression* of culture under particular material conditions and its underlying *logic*.[1] The pattern of human relationships implies an underlying mechanism or logic of social interaction that is perhaps expressed in different ways under different material conditions. The *expression* of those relationships on the web, for example, need not imply a fundamental transformation of the *logic* of human relationships. Similarly, while the *expression* of art changes in response to changing artistic media, the migration of art into digital forms need be no more indicative of the transformation of the *logic* of artistic practice than the introduction of different pigments of oil paints. Culture, perhaps, allows many more modes of expression than are ever actually realised, in the same way that languages allow the infinite production of original utterances. We perhaps possess a *culture instinct* akin to Pinker's (1994) *language instinct*, or a universal cultural grammar akin to Chomsky's (1957) universal language grammar. But with this approach we soon run into difficulties. It is unclear what *culture* means if it is separated from the forms, practices, traditions and beliefs through which it finds expression. We may have secured the idea of culture against a simple relationship with the material conditions of its production, but only at the expense of a concept that can be analysed. Furthermore, it remains no clearer how the material conditions under which culture is expressed themselves influence the nature of that expression. We have arrived at a solution that apparently puts culture beyond analysis, but leaves the original problem intact. In the process we have been drawn into an accidental idealism that disassociates culture and material reality.

If *culture* must therefore represent something more than the intangible essence of cultural practices and social relations, need it necessarily represent something entirely different from the material conditions of its own production? Could what we call culture be simply an affect of our social lives, a kind of second-hand quality arising merely as a by-product of social relations? Another way of putting this is to ask whether culture and technology are really different kinds of things that we can hold in contrast, or whether culture is just a way of describing the way in which technology, social relationships, economic structures and everything else we might want to include within our nebulous understanding of culture *play out* against each other over time within a social system. Perhaps culture as a distinct idea can be altogether excised. But there is a danger in this idea of petrifying culture by transforming it into an affect of everyday matter in a way that is perhaps too dogmatically materialist. While isolating culture from the material conditions of its production can lead to a cascade into idealism, treating culture as merely the expression of those material conditions conversely tends to lead to technological determinism. If culture is nothing other than the expression of the material conditions under which it is produced, then we should be able to read from those material conditions a description of culture. This undermines the role of human agency. While we should not want to abandon the idea that culture is in some way grounded in the material conditions of cultural production, neither should we want to reduce culture to merely an affect of those conditions.

These two opposing arguments illustrate how different ideas about what culture is and how it is formed also influence how the relationship between technology and culture is framed and understood. Whichever way we turn, the discourse of culture and technology tends to become inadvertently ensnared by either dogmatic materialism leading to technological determinism or a denial of culture's sensitivity to technological development, and ultimately a denial that culture is in any of its many senses determined by the material conditions of its production and an evaporation of the material basis of culture into idealism. This is in part a consequence of how we situate ourselves within the discourse of culture and technology: whether we start with technology and work back to culture, or start with culture and work forward to technology. Discussion around the information age, and around digital culture, invariably chooses to start with the idea of technology and map it on to whatever sense of 'culture' will fit. Most of the cultural tradition encountered in Chapter 1 chooses the second approach, starting with the idea of culture and trying to situate the influence of technology within it. But it is also a consequence of how we understand the relationship between the real and the abstract, or the material and the ideal. Larrain (1979: 38) has commented that 'while materialism makes consciousness a reflection of external reality, idealism makes reality the product of consciousness', and this is exactly the issue that faces us. We may insist on the interplay of culture and technology, or on an eternal balance of influences complicit in the mechanism of social change, but that insistence often conceals the drift towards idealism and determinism rather than overcoming it.

While the dilemma of determinism is one of the most intractable problems in the sociology of technology, by concentrating critical attention on questions of causation it also obscures the other ways in which culture and technology are enmeshed. Both culture and technology are implicated in the social processes and therefore complicit in our experience of change. But technological change and its socio-cultural consequences are also themselves the subject of cultural expression and experimentation. Because of its reflexive action, cultural critique becomes a part of the cultural field. How we understand culture and its relationship with technology is also a part of our cultural outlook. This book will argue that problems like the dilemma of determinism emerge not from the objective relationship between technology and culture, but from the ways we subjectively frame, describe and represent that relationship between these two significantly indistinct and liquid ideas. How we experience the agency of technology over society and culture reflects in part the influence of our prepossession with that relationship. The way in which technology is represented as an agent of socio-cultural change is also complicit in our apprehension and experience of that change.

This is a complex idea that will be examined in two parts over two chapters. This chapter explores the ways in which technology is represented within different kinds of discourses, from academic works to fiction, film, television and the popular press. Although these different kinds of discourse seek to do very different things, there nevertheless emerge through them certain dominant themes in the representation of technology, certain common ways of describing and explaining its influence and agency. This chapter explores some of these tropes: authenticity, alienation, decline, transgression, emancipation and spatial-temporal drift. The following chapter will explore just how these representations of technology shape and condition our experience of change.

Representations of technology

What does it mean to be human in the technological age? One of the most unsettling commentaries on questions of the authenticity of identity under conditions of technological change can be found in the work of the American science-fiction writer Philip K. Dick – called by Ursula LeGuin 'America's Borges' (Disch, [1986] 1991: 10). His novels and short stories have reached mass audiences in film adaptations such as *Total Recall* (1990), *Minority Report* (2002) and *Screamers* (1995). They have also influenced social theorists such as Baudrillard, and post-modernist critiques of the body and cybernetics. None quite does justice to the haunting paranoia and insecurity of Dick's fiction. His most famous work, *Do Androids Dream of Electric Sheep?* (1972), was adapted for film as *Blade Runner* (1982). Within its world, humans and androids are distinguishable only through the use of psychometric tests that measure empathetic and emotional responses. Androids yearn after the debris of emotional lives, such as photographs and keepsakes, without being able to access their emotional resonance. Conversely, the authenticity of human experiences is undermined by the technological manipulation of emotion and empathy through *mood organs*. The book ends with Rick Deckard's discovery of a toad in the desert which he assumes to be real. When his wife, Iran, finds a control panel on the belly of the toad, Deckard responds simply 'I'm glad to know, or rather – [...] I'd prefer to know' (Dick, 1972: 182). In the book more explicitly than the film, Deckard's doubts about his own humanity permeate the story; his emotional emptiness by the end of the novel hints at his own uncertainty. Dick blurs the boundaries between human and machine.

Throughout his work, Dick draws out anxieties about the authenticity of experience and memory in the face of simulation, and the tendency for technology to blur the real and unreal. The undermining of experiential authenticity is an effect widely attributed to technology within popular culture, fiction and film. In *Brave New World* (1932), Aldous Huxley described a future in which both individuality is erased and emotion manipulated through recreational drug use and 'feelies' – an extension of and commentary on cinema. The central character of John the Savage functions as an outside observer on the technological society, representing human nature in its unblemished natural state. When he objects that '*Othello*'s better than those feelies', the World Controller for Western Europe replies:

> Of course it is [...] But that's the price we have to pay for stability. You've got to choose between happiness and what people used to call high art. We've sacrificed high art. We have the feelies and scent organ instead. (Huxley, 1932: 219)

Huxley explores the moral ambiguity of happiness contrasted with emotional authenticity. The population of the World State are indocrtinated into happiness; 'sixty-two thousand four hundred repetitions make one truth' (ibid.: 60). Similar themes are explored in the films *Vanilla Sky* (2001) and *The Matrix* trilogy (1999, 2003), in which forms of simulation replace real life and the value of authentic experience remains uncertain. In *Being John Malkovich* (1999) the effects of media technology are parodied by literally placing the protagonists inside the head of the performer; the marionette theme running through the film captures the danger of the subjugation of identity under the weight of media control. The reliability of memory is questioned in films including *Eternal Sunshine of the Spotless Mind* (2004) and *Total Recall* (1990), where technological manipulation undermines the certainty of remembered pasts. These very different works all play out the contested nature of human identity under conditions of technological simulation. When experience can be simulated or erased, the ontological security of being comes under question. Technological advancement therefore poses questions about the boundaries of experience, emotion and freedom under the subjugation of the individual to the demands of the machine.

A related idea is that technology changes not only what it means to be human, but also what *human* is. By intervening in the make-up of our bodies, technology perhaps threatens the erasure of biology. The Polish satirical film *Seksmisja*[2] (1984) presents a technological future in which procreation and sex have become divorced, leading to the eradication of men. In *The Island* (2005) human cloning leads to the farming of humans for replacement body-parts. *Children of Men* (2006) presents a dystopian vision of a world torn apart by the catastrophic decline in human fertility. The American film *Gattaca* (1998) explores a future in which routine genetic engineering has resulted in new forms of social division, the genetically flawless children of the wealthy dominating over an underclass subject to congenital or progressive conditions. Similar anxieties filter through popular culture in the debates around genetic modification, cloning research and the human genome project. Through technology we perhaps become gradually distanced from our animal nature.

Other works explore the nature of the body under conditions of technological manipulation. In William Gibson's *Neuromancer* (1984) body modification, in pursuit of both an aesthetic ideal derived more from technology than from nature and the enhancement of the body's normal range of functioning, is routine. Molly, a recurring character in Gibson's works, is described early in the book:

> The glasses were surgically inset. The silver lenses seemed to grow from the smooth pale skin above her cheekbones [...] She held out her hands, palms up, the white fingers slightly spread, and with a barely audible click, ten double edged, four centimetre scalpel blades slid from their housing beneath the burgundy nails. (Gibson, 1984: 36–7).

Neuromancer echoes other works of fiction, from Mary Shelley's *Frankenstein* ([1885] 1992) to Wells's *The Invisible Man* (1938), and television programmes such as *The Six Million Dollar Man* (1974–1978). But in Gibson's work technological enhancement is presented as a bleak fulfilment of market-driven aesthetic trends and fashions. In films like *Johnny Mnemonic* (1995)[3] and *Tron* (1982) the human and the machine begin to merge. In recent years these ideas have become increasingly important to social theory, developed through discourses on the nature of the body in the digital age, and around ideas such as the cyborg and the post-human. The limits of human nature under conditions of technological change shape how we think about our own bodies and their relationship to the social environment. As technology advances, the distinction between the body and the machine breaks down. We engage in a gradual migration of human nature until we become indistinguishable, perhaps, from the machine.

The sense that technology undermines human identity draws on more explicit anxieties about technology's dehumanising and alienating effects. Alienation describes the idea that technology divorces us from both our true selves and our true social relationships. Instead of liberating us from work, technology strips human relationships of their emotional value. In an increasingly advanced technological society, we become severed from real lived experience, sealed off in controlled environments, moments of agony and ecstasy dulled into an extended evenness of experience. Technology sanitises death and illness. It removes pain, hunger and fear. It creates in us false desires, needs and memories, undermining our social relationships and subjecting us to phantasms of friendship, lust, love and enmity through pulp fiction, cinema, television and pornography. In the digital world we become subject to the endless procession of digital chimeras, losing touch with our true selves and shared social values, eternally chasing the ghosts of the machine.

Alienation in the sociology of technology originates in the work of Karl Marx. Before Marx, Ludwig Andreas Feuerbach had argued that mankind projected on to the idea of god a set of values that were essentially human, but which created a false opposition between our spiritual and physical being resulting in the alienation of individuals from their own true state of being. Marx adapted this idea and applied it to the structures of capitalist production, arguing that both the industrial process and industrial machinery alienate by creating a false opposition of work and being that results in the reification of work and the subjugation of the individual to the demands of industrial production.[4] By losing self-determination in their working lives, individuals become alienated from their own true nature. This idea of the alienating effect of technology emerges in the critique of Horkheimer and Adorno ([1944] 2006: 42), who described technological rationalism as 'the compulsive character of a society alienated from itself'. Individuals are subjugated to the rhythm of the machine.

Alienation also arises in the sociology of technology in quite a different sense: from the qualities of technologically mediated communication itself. Those technologies that at face value have had the most significant impact on culture and society all act to facilitate, extend and transform human communication: the printing press, radio, television, cinema, video games, the internet and the World Wide Web, mobile phones, WiFi and so on. Each sits in the spaces between people, both framing and reconstructing communication along the lines of their own structural rules and logic. Each therefore filters sensory perception and reconstructs lived experience out of very partial representations. The telephone reduces communication to the single channel of the voice. Film and television flatten perception and reconstruct lived experience in images and sound. Web forums mediate communication through the written word. Immersive simulated environments disembody the subject. In this process they perhaps tend to both distance us from social relations and replace lived experience with various forms of representation and simulation. Leavis ([1930] 2006: 14), for example, described the influence of film as involving the 'surrender, under conditions of hypnotic receptivity, to the cheapest emotional appeals, appeals all the more insidious because they are associated with a compellingly vivid illusion of actual life'. Horkheimer and Adorno ([1944] 2006: 45) argued that 'film denies its audience any dimension in which they might roam free in imagination [...] it trains those exposed to it to identify film directly with reality'. McLuhan's (1964: 24) analysis turned on the extent to which different media and communications technologies extend 'one single sense in high definition' and 'allow of less participation' (ibid.: 25). As technologically mediated communication becomes more important to the way in which we live our lives, its partial representations increasingly replace real lived experience, leaving us feeling detached and emotionally flat.

This alienating effect of technology is a significant theme in the popular discourse of culture and technology: iPods divorce us from our social surrounding; video games replace lived experience with emotionally hollow simulated encounters; social networking sites replace real social relationships. Through our use of technology we become locked in emotional prisons of our own making. One dominant example of this effect attributed to technology is the changing experience of childhood. For about the last 30 years, different technologies from television, video nasties, computer games, games consoles and more recently chat sites, SMS and iPods have been widely held to have contributed to the progressive deterioration of childhood experiences and childhood innocence. These three quotations from UK national newspapers reflect some of this anxiety.

> Today's prison-house is just as likely to be the home, a seductive, comfortable prison for boys and girls whose nimble little fingers are adept at working their mobiles and computer games, but who've never used them to play conkers. (Connolly, 2007)

> Childhood is being 'poisoned' by a culture of junk food, marketing, video games and school targets, experts have warned. Rapid technological advances and a lack of interaction with 'real-life' adults – as opposed to via a computer screen – are leading to a rise in the number of children suffering psychological and behavioural problems. (Roberts, 2006)

> Children are apparently more miserable than ever before [...] The recreational play their parents enjoyed has been displaced by computer games and television. (*The Daily Telegraph*, 2006)

In this anxiety we can perhaps recognise both the influence of very real social change and a nostalgic idealisation of childhood. But there is also the echo of a more persistent theme about the nature of technology and culture, a theme that knits those concerns into a broader narrative about the social impact of technology. The idea of alienation provides a framework into which anxieties about different kinds of social change can be slotted.

What happens to culture under conditions of technological change? Like alienation, the idea of decline focuses on the perceived negative effects of technological advancement, predicating a general decline in culture, social standards or moral values. With each new wave of technology comes a progressive decline in cultural values and attainment. The steam press reduced literature to mass-produced paperbacks and pulp magazines. Cinema undermined popular reading of literature and poetry. Television threatened to destroy the cinema. And so on.

Technology has often been associated with cultural decline in this way. Indeed, the very idea of culture and its performative, reflective function was partially forged out of anxieties induced by industrialisation and the growth of mass publishing. Arnold was in little doubt that industry had led to a decline in cultural values, writing:

> If England were swallowed up by the sea to-morrow, which of the two, a hundred years hence, would most excite the love, interest and admiration of mankind, – would most, therefore, show the evidences of having possessed greatness, – the England of the last twenty years, or the England of Elizabeth? (Arnold, 1869: 18)

His appropriation of the idea of culture confronted this perceived social and cultural impact of technology. Leavis ([1930] 2006: 17) lamented the 'desperate plight' and 'levelling down' of culture resulting from the new media of cinema and radio, and the 'smother of new books'. Eliot (1948: 19) insisted that 'we can assert with some confidence that our own period is one of decline'.

The fear of socio-cultural decline may be particularly associated with the culture and civilisation tradition, but it is also a more persistent theme within the wider discourse of culture and technology. It perhaps represents a normal mode of engagement with the anxiety of change, a resting point against which all technological advancement tends to be evaluated. Decline is implicit within the culture industry critique of Horkheimer and Adorno ([1944] 2006), who see in emerging technology only a caricature of culture. Some aspects of Hoggart's (1957) analysis of the early post-war years are haunted by regret about the loss of traditional forms and practices. When Postman (1992) explored the impact of digital technologies, he was unable to escape the allure of a cultural decline; the power of technology was to transform society and culture in ways both positive and negative, but Postman is always drawn by the negative aspects of technological change. More recently, the fear of cultural decline is manifest in Keen's delineation of the *Cult of the Amateur* (2007) and McDonald's *The Death of the Critic* (2007). The idea of decline feeds into dystopian fiction, film and television, such as Wells's *The Time Machine* (1895), Vonnegut's *Player Piano* (1953) and *Galapagos* (1985), Orwell's *1984* (1949), Zamyatin's *We* (1972) and Atwood's *The Handmaid's Tale* (1985). And lingering behind many newspaper and television news headlines is the present anxiety that everything is getting worse. In September 2006, for example, the BBC published a survey reporting that half of Britons believed that things are less good now than in 1986 (BBC, 2006). A year later another BBC poll indicated that more than 80 per cent of the population believed moral standards were in decline (BBC, 2007). Fear of moral and cultural decline asserts itself at every opportunity.

Decline generally turns on a set of general social effects that are ascribed to technologies of different kinds. Printing, industrialisation, cinema, television, video nasties, computer games and massively multiplayer role-playing games are all attributed with the same general effects: a promotion of quantity above quality, a weakening of discrimination, an enfeebling of the mind, a lack of acquaintance with tradition, a confusion of moral values, a corruption of the spirit, a decline in honesty and decency, an encouragement of selfishness and individualism, a homogenisation of culture and so on. These same general effects tend to be attributed to very different kinds of technology, from the jukebox and contraception in the work of Hoggart to the printing press in the work of Adorno. In 1477 Hieronimo Squarciafico wrote that the 'abundance of books makes men less studious'; it destroys memory and enfeebles the mind by relieving it of too much work (cited by Ong, 1982: 79). Over 400 years later, Postman (1992: xii) argued that technology 'creates a culture without a moral foundation' and 'undermines certain mental processes and social relations that make human life worth living'. The technology may change, but its perceived impact remains largely the same.

How does technology change the ethical dimension of human lives? Many kinds of technical innovation pose moral and ethical questions. The advancement of stem-cell research and the treatment of progressive illnesses both force us to confront the threshold of viable human life. Genetic engineering poses questions about human intervention in 'natural' processes. Theoretical physics and engineering put destructive power in our hands, and moral obligations relating to its use. There is a sense that technology outpaces our existing moral and ethical frameworks; we are perhaps living with a nineteenth-century moral framework in a twenty-first-century world. The treatment of the ethical dimension of technological change is often haunted by a real ambivalence, the perception of benefits and risks in balance. Postman (1992: 4–5), for example, argued that 'every technology is both a burden and a blessing; not either-or but this-and-that'. Freud ([1930] 2002) believed that technology often only solves the problems that it itself created.

The ethical dilemma of technological change arises in part from the perceived erasure of human values in the automation of human social processes. Because technologies intervene in human social processes, they tend to replace decision-making with automated processes and distance human action from the site of its effect. The action to launch a guided missile is more distanced from its effect than the action to fire a rifle. Flaming a discussion forum[5] is more distanced from its effect than haranguing a public meeting. As a consequence, mechanised processes perhaps become detached from the ethical and moral sphere. This is an anxiety explicit in many cultural representations of technology, from *Dr. Strangelove* (1964) to *WarGames* (1983) and *The Matrix* trilogy (1999, 2003). In the film *Soylent Green* (1973), for example, the fear of overpopulation is transformed into a moral ambivalence towards the human body and its use as a foodstuff arising from the automation of food production.

Equally, technological change is often represented as a kind of Promethean transgression against the natural order, a theft of fire from the gods. Technology becomes both alluring and insidious, bringing great gains but drawing us into traps of hubris and self-delusion. Mary Shelley's *Frankenstein* ([1885] 1992), which has been called the first work of science fiction (Aldiss, 1973), epitomises this idea. Early in the book, Frankenstein records:

> It was the secrets of heaven and earth that I desired to learn; and whether it was the outward substance of things, or the inner spirit of nature and the mysterious soul of man that occupied me, still my enquiries were directed towards the metaphysical, or in its highest sense, the physical secrets of the world. (Shelley, [1885] 1992: 37)

Shelley explores the hubris of the scientific conquest of nature, pitting a deontological ethical outlook against a form of consequentialism where Frankenstein's tragedy arises from the both the outcome and the aspiration of his endeavours. Science and technology teeter on the edge of control, reflecting perhaps anxieties about nineteenth-century advances in science and medicine just as vivid as modern-day anxieties about genetic engineering. John Wyndham's cosy catastrophes develop similar themes; *The Trouble with Lichen* (1960) for example exploring the vanity of medicine's pursuit of immortality. Works of this kind explore the hubris of the human desire for both knowledge and mastery over nature. What start out as good intentions spiral out of control.

Another kind of fear draws on the transgressions of Narcissus and Pygmalion. Through technology we become subject to the lure of both our own creations and our own reflection in those creations. In fiction, film and television, machine intelligence is a recurring theme; just a few examples are Hal in *2001: A Space Odyssey* (1968), Data in *Star Trek: The Next Generation* (1987–1994), Orax and Zen in *Blake's Seven* (1978–1991), Holly in *Red Dwarf* (1988–1999), C3P0 and R2D2 in the *Star Wars* series (1977–1983), WOPR in *WarGames* (1983), the ship's computer and the onboard bomb in *Dark Star* (1974), Skynet in *The Terminator* films (1985–2003) and the androids in Asimov's *I Robot* stories (1950). Sometimes machine intelligence is represented as a threat and at other times it is benign, but always it exposes anxieties about human identity, human culture and the limits of human reasoning. Technology challenges our monopoly on sentience and reasoned action. But the persistent theme of machine intelligence also perhaps reflects the narcissistic nature of technological development; in technology we see our own image reflected, and sometimes it proves to be both abhorrent and alluring. The danger of the machine is also the desire for knowledge of human nature.

How does technology change the spaces within which we live? Many theorists have argued that communications technologies warp, distort or cheat both space and time. Writing about the impact of printing, Mumford ([1947] 2007: 94) argued that 'it increased every man's range in time and space, bringing together distant times past and times to come, near and distant, peoples long dead and peoples still unborn'. Freud ([1930] 2002: 31) described the 'newly won mastery over space and time' of the industrial age. McLuhan (1962, 1964) coined the idea of the 'global village' to describe the collapsing of physical space initiated by media technology. More recently Castells (2000) has described the 'space of flows' and 'timeless time' that result from networked digital computers. Writing, printing, film and digital computing both bring the past closer to the present and create a time outside of time. Serial asynchronous communications generate their own temporal frame independent of chronological time; the shrinking of the globe means that it is always all times everywhere. Technology is also often blamed for an acceleration of culture. Leavis ([1930] 2006: 13) argued that technology 'has brought about change in habit and the circumstances of life at a rate for which we have no parallel'. Gleick's *Faster* (1999) explores the idea of acceleration across the social and cultural world. As culture speeds up an increasingly ephemeral quality of experience asserts itself, a disposable culture in which immediacy replaces longer-term aspirations, relationships and concerns.

Another part of technology's effect on our social environment emerges in its distorting or telescoping effect. Media and communications technologies such as the telegraph, telephone, television and internet draw together distant places, improving the efficacy and potency of action and agency over distance. They also perhaps allow new forms of social organisation that come to replace traditional social structures built around physical proximity. Toffler (1980) coined the phrase 'electronic cottage' to describe technology's potential effect on the future of work. More recently Castells (2000, 2001, 2004) has described the 'network society', in which new forms of community emerge though the influence of networked digital computers. In addition digital technologies create *other* or *virtual* space carved outside of the material world in the spaces between spaces. This is the environment of Castells's 'space of flows' (2000), Gibson's cyberspace (1984) and *The Matrix* (1999). It is the environment of social networking sites, discussion forums, massively multiplayer role-playing games such as *World of Warcraft* (1994) and *Myst* (1993), and social worlds such as *Second Life* (2003). It is the environment of the holodeck in *Star Trek: The Next Generation* (1987–1994), and of 'Better than Life' in *Red Dwarf* (1988–1999). In the disembodied dreamscape of the virtual simulated environment, we cast off the constraints of the material world.

These ways of representing the effects of technological change highlight how technology seems to change the context of human action and human experience, and perhaps inevitably as a result changes our values and aspirations. Political movements such as anti-war or environmental groupings organise simultaneous protests in different continents. More threateningly, terrorists have become more global not only in organisation but also in action. As a consequence of our ability to partake in transnational social networks and organisations, the importance of local communities and of nation-states seems to decline. Much of the anxiety over the influence of digital computing has been linked to the impact of technology on traditional communities and traditional forms of social organisation, from the neighbourhood to the extended family. The decline in geographically constrained cultural identity is sometimes represented as a fragmentation of culture, as in some post-modernist theory, and sometimes as a homogenising of culture, as in the work of the Frankfurt School, the McDonaldisation of culture proposed by Ritzer (1996) and the commodification of information identified by Schiller (1976, 1986).

If the representations of technology considered so far tend to contribute to a rather bleak picture, there is some respite in the theme of technological emancipation. It encloses the idea that technological advancement is always liberating, leading to a progressive betterment of the human condition. Many theorists cannot help falling in love with the gleam of new technologies; even those we would otherwise imagine might know better. Horkheimer and Adorno ([1944] 2006), for example, combine a rejection of the culture industry with a maudlin modernist fascination with the technologies on which it depends. And many theorists allow that fascination to spill over into unrequited optimism. Perhaps the most explicit versions of this in popular culture come through certain forms of science fiction: the space operas of Robert Heinlein and their television equivalent in *Star Trek*. But this kind of narrative is also associated with the popular sociology of technology, particularly in the works of Alvin Toffler and Nicholas Negroponte. Fukuyama's *The End of History* (1989, 1992) clearly argues the progressive directional nature of technological development. These works tends to focus on a range of related issues: technology expands the compass of human experience, reduces the drudgery and agony of life, vanquishes the fear of isolation and gives meaning to life. By releasing us from certain constraints of the physical world, technology has led to a general betterment of the human condition.

Representations and reality

This chapter has touched on a number of different representations of the influence of technology on the individual, society and culture: questions of identity, alienation, decline, Promethean transgression, emancipation, spatial and temporal drift and so on. These persistent themes do not exhaust the ways in which technology is represented in different kinds of discourse, but they are indicative of some dominant tropes. About them one can note a number of things. In the first case, such representations transcend particular kinds of discourse; the representations of technology contained in film and fiction share characteristics with, and largely reflect the same anxieties as, those in the popular press or in theoretical works. Secondly, they transcend particular kinds of technology; the anxieties attached to genetic engineering are not so very different from those attached to nineteenth-century medicine; both printing and the internet reduce space and time. Thirdly one can note that they are broadly speaking negative, emphasising the dangers of technological change over the benefits that accrue from that change. This persistent negativity in the representation of technology is somewhat counterintuitive to our experiences; we perhaps tend to feel that the modern age is one of tremendous celebration of the power and potency of technology. It is better characterised as an age of immense anxiety about the boundaries between the technological and the human. This discrepancy needs some explanation, which will be addressed in the following chapter.

There is a tendency perhaps to think of the relationship of culture and technology operating in only one direction, technological advances influencing the cultural representation of technology but not vice versa. An impression of this may have been given through this chapter. However, technological innovation is not independent of the cultural sphere. The discourse of culture and technology tends to run ahead of technological change, exploring unrealised possibilities and threats. How technology is represented in fiction, film and popular culture, as well as in sociological and cultural theory, sets out a kind of field of possibilities within which technological development takes place. For any particular innovation we can find foreshadows in the cultural sphere. Wells's 'world brain' (1937), Vannevar Bush's 'As we may think' (1945), Borges's 'library of Babel' (1962) and Nelson's Xanadu project (2000) all suggest their own realisation in the World Wide Web. The personal communicators in *Star Wars*, *Blake's Seven* and countless other science-fiction films and television shows find their own realisation in mobile telephony. Arthur C. Clarke (1945) famously predicted the communications satellite. None of these is a perfect match; the direct link that is often claimed between the emergence of these ideas in fiction and discourse and their realisation in the technological does not really exist. Just as cultural representations of technology are not merely reflections of innovation, neither is innovation merely a reflection of the ideas explored in the cultural sphere. The assimilation of technical possibility through culture becomes part of a complex process of innovation and change.

More than anything, these representations reveal the anxieties associated with technological change. That they retain their relevance long after the technologies to which they refer have become obsolete and the particular anxieties they express have subsided highlights how they tap into more fundamental qualities of experience. The persistent nature of certain core themes through very different kinds of discourse, applied to very different kinds of technology, suggests that they appertain not to particular experiences of change, but to general anxieties associated with technology and its effects. They expose the unfamiliarity of advancement and the fears that unfamiliarity brings. With technological change we become perhaps like children in the dark of the night, our imaginations running wild, conjuring all manner of present dangers ahead of daybreak. In the following chapter it will be argued that the way in which we describe technology and its effects has an important influence on how we experience those effects. Representations of technology are not neutral reflections of an objective reality, but complicit in our experiences of technological change.

Notes

1. 'Logic' is here used in the rather loose sense of an underlying system of constraints and potentials in human behaviour.
2. English title: *Sex Mission.*
3. Based on a short story of the same name by William Gibson (1986).
4. Feuerbach develops the idea of alienation in *The Essence of Christianity* ([1841] 1957); see also Larrain (1979: 31–4).
5. Defined by the *Oxford English Dictionary* (2001) as 'The action or practice of sending inflammatory, abusive, or (occas.) inconsequential messages by e-mail or as a posting to a newsgroup, freq. in an impulsively angry response to a previous message or a perceived breach of Internet etiquette.'

3

Narratives of technology and culture

This chapter explores the role of narrative in the discourse of culture and technology. It will argue that how we experience the effects of technology on culture and society is in part a matter of the ways in which we frame and articulate those effects within the cultural sphere. The representations of technology explored in the previous chapter are complicit in the experience of a radical shift in social life accompanying the digital age. It is not simply the case that by obsessing over particular forms of technological influence and agency we begin to see their effects manifested and reproduced within every facet of the socio-cultural world, although this is an important aspect of a wider issue. Rather it will be argued that to discuss change is always to frame and situate the experience of change within narratives. Narrative forms mediate and contain our apprehension of technology's agency in the experience of socio-cultural transformation.

Narrative structures

The idea that narrative plays some fundamental role in the way in which people describe their experiences has become more important within social theory in recent years. Chandler (2002: 90) has observed that 'turning experience into narratives seems to be a fundamental feature of the human drive to make meaning'. Similarly, Morson (1994: 19) has written that 'one way in which people explain the world is by telling stories about it, and so to grasp *how* stories explain is to understand our own methods of understanding'. To describe representations of technology within theoretical and popular discourse as examples of narrative is therefore to construct their meaning in one particular way, but a way that helps explain how we make sense of our experiences. In particular it marks a distinction between two modes of thought; two different ways of deriving meaning from experience. The logico-scientific or rationalist mode 'attempts to fulfil the ideal of a formal mathematic system of description and explanation' (Bruner, 1986: 12). This is the methodological outlook of science and much social research. By contrast, the narrative mode 'deals in human or human-like intention and action and the vicissitudes and consequences that mark their course. It strives to put its timeless miracles into the particulars of experience, and to locate experience in time and place' (ibid.: 13). Narratives provide a holistic and non-analytical means of assimilating and describing experience. The truths to which they aspire are not analytic, but pertain to human understanding and emotion.

Narratives of culture and technology are simply the different kinds of stories we tell as a way of making sense of our experience in the digital age. To call them stories is not to imply their lack of seriousness; such narratives have a powerful hold over the way in which we apprehend technological innovation. Many of the accounts of social and cultural change come in explicit narrative form: novels, films, drama and television. It has been noted that these become complicit in technological innovation. But many analytical accounts of technological change also share characteristics of narratives. Principally they assimilate our experience of change: cause and effect; the temporal sequence of events; and the movement from one state of affairs to another. The kind of social change on which they concentrate is that which is associated with technological advancement. They also tend to exhibit selectivity in the phenomena, ideas and relationships on which they focus; an appeal to basic mythic ideas and forms; and a construction of particular relationships between aspects of technology and culture. This chapter will explore how these characteristics influence the way in which we experience socio-cultural change.

Bennett and Royle (1999: 54) observe that narratives 'always involve self-reflexive and metafictional dimensions'; they always tell us something about how we construct the world in narrative form. Narratives give structure to experience by coordinating disparate ideas and events, and creating meaningful relationships between them. One means by which they achieve this is through their construction out of experience of what Morson (1994: 22) has called *eventness*:

> For there to be eventness, there must be alternatives. Eventful events are performed in a world in which there are multiple possibilities, in which some things that could happen do not. In such a world, time ramifies and its possibilities multiply; each realized possibility opens new choices while precluding others that once could have been made.

Narrative events possess temporality (they occur in time), directionality (they occur in sequence), causation (they are linked with one another), meaningfulness (they are attributed significance; they explain something) and scope (they are limited in space and time). They become meaningful by forging causal relationships that fit into particular narrative frameworks. They therefore contain only those aspects of experience that fit particular patterns of change. Chandler (2002: 90) observes that 'there are no "events" in the world. Reality cannot be reduced objectively to discrete temporal units; what counts as an "event" is determined by one's purposes.' The apparent eventness of our experience is a product of our tendency to understand the world by recourse to narrative structures.

Because the meaningfulness of narrative events is determined by their relationship to one another in sequence, the creation of eventness always implies a filtering of experience through linear narrative structures. How we understand change both precedes and derives from the transformation of experience into eventness. We should therefore expect narratives of culture and technology to display a high degree of selectivity in the phenomena on which they concentrate and which they seek to explain. This is exactly what we find. It is difficult to maintain a consistent belief in decline, morphological drift or alienation other than by reference to selective accounts of social change. We can list particular phenomena that fit each of these narrative lines well enough: examples of cultural decline in the wake of technological advancement, alienation as an effect of media technology, technology as an agent of the surveillance society and so on. But in each case we can also list counterexamples that undermine these accounts. It is not in their ability to explain and describe particular kinds of change that these narratives wield their power, but in their tendency to move from those particular kinds of change to assertions about the general quality of culture in the face of technological advancement. Through their selectiveness, narratives join the dots of disparate kinds of experience. What genetic engineering, the steam press, atomic energy, plastic surgery, digital computers and the web have in common is that we can contain them within narratives of decline, transgression, alienation, morphological drift or emancipation. The transitory nature of these correlations, and the intransigence of narrative logic in the face of exceptions, tends to disarm any dissent against the explanations of change they contain. Thus these narrative formations do not pertain to analytical truths arising through induction from a consideration of the detail of experience, but to ways of understanding and assimilating change that prefigure the particular examples of technology to which they are applied.

The idea that narrative forms prefigure the experience of change recalls the mythopoeic function of culture. In coordinating eventness into experience, the different narratives explored here draw on basic mythic structures that pertain to the assimilation of more general ontological and existential angst. The anxiety of cultural and social decline, for example, haunts the Western intellectual tradition, and is attributed to many different causes. In 63 BC Cicero declared 'O tempora! O mores!'; the times and the customs were in a lamentable state, on account of political intrigue and unrest. In the 1380s the English poet John Gower identified social and cultural decline with irreligiousness and rebellion (Gower, [c. 1390] 1900: Prologue). Starn (1975: 1) notes: 'From Hesiod and Thucydides to St Augustine and Orosius, Rousseau and Gibbon, Nietzsche and Burckhardt, Spengler and Huizinga, some of the most significant historical speculation and narrative have been phrased in terms of decline.'

Any one of these examples can be attributed to the particular social conditions of the age in which it was formed, but taken together they paint a bleak picture of a constant and gradual decay. Decline does not become consistently applied to the impact of technology until the industrial revolution, and even after that time it continues also to be associated with other kinds of social change. Today, cultural decline is linked to educational standards, crime, urbanisation, the destruction of the countryside, the state of youth culture and any number of other sources of social tension. Comparing these different forms, one finds that they tend to focus on the same kinds of anxieties and turn on the same kinds of issues. This suggests that the idea of decay does not describe something specifically related to our apprehension of technological change, but instead expresses general tensions and anxieties manifest in many kinds of social change. The logic of the narrative structures our understanding and apprehension of change in the social world.

Similar conclusions can be drawn in relation to other narratives of culture and technology. Alienation is explicit in the Genesis myth, underpins Satan's tragedy in Milton's ([1667] 1968) *Paradise Lost* and recurs throughout Western culture. Morphological change emerges in Ovid's *Metamorphosis,* in fairy stories and in Kafka's *Metamorphosis* ([1916] 1961). The dangerous trangressive nature of knowledge is explicit in both the Faustus myth and medieval debates on alchemy. The reiteration of existing themes forms part of the mythic texture of the narratives of culture and technology; each draws on wellsprings of imagery and ideas to coordinate our understanding of social and cultural change. Through this deployment of existing narrative forms, general anxieties reflecting ontological and existential angst are projected on to particular manifestations of change. Morson (1994: 22) observes that 'received narrative forms do not just find the meaning of events, they also – some would say only – smuggle meaning into events, at times cynically but often unawares'. The prototypal narrative forms that mediate our apprehension of technological and social change draw us towards conclusions that are the outcome of the narrative structures themselves, rather than the outcome of technological change.

Is there any particular explanation for this recourse to mythic themes to explain the impact of technology? Postman (1992: 58) comments: 'the world we live in is very nearly incomprehensible to most of us'. He notes that one of the consequences of the advancement of technology is a distancing of experience from explanatory frameworks. Arthur C. Clarke (1973: 21) famously commented that 'any sufficiently advanced technology is indistinguishable from magic'. This captures the wonder of technological innovation, which constantly vanquishes the impossibilities of the past. Myths come to mind perhaps because the mythic captures the impossibility of technological achievement. However, this explanation is incomplete. Our ability to explain the working of the television set, for example, is perhaps no more essential to our experience of *television* than was Plato's ability to explain the working of the Oracle of Delphi to his faith in its revelations. The strangeness with which technology confronts us is not essentially different from the strangeness of other aspects of experience. Postman (1992) overemphasises the rationalist desire to explain analytically and contain every aspect of lived experience.

The mythic and the technological intertwine because narratives of technology and culture are principally concerned not with technology but with human values. And while technologies change, the anxieties of human experience tend to remain the same. Although superficially addressing the effects of particular kinds of change, narratives of culture and technology address more general anxieties pertaining to mutable experience. Culture becomes susceptible to integration into narratives of this kind precisely because it contains its own mythopoeic function. It has been argued that culture replaced other shared meaning systems and values undermined by the encroachment of science and technology. By remaining beyond articulation and subject to negotiation, culture provided a mechanism for assimilating different aspects of experience without reconciling their contradictions. It refracts and distils the experience of different kinds of social change: industrialisation, diasporas, urbanisation and post-industrial capitalism. Technology becomes not the cause of these anxieties but the vehicle for their expression, and culture the means of framing, fixing and stabilising the values against which its agency is effected.

Forms and imagery

Bennett and Royle (1999: 54) suggest that 'not only do we tell stories, but stories tell us'. The narratives of culture and technology are not mirrors of experience, but participants in the construction of experience out of the building blocks of story-telling. One way in which they mould our understanding of things is by smuggling meaning into events by carving up experience into discrete categories. The different narratives of culture and technology explored in the preceding chapter all construct binary oppositions that create antithetical relationships between different aspects of experience: culture and technology; progress and regression; nature and artifice; human and non-human; reality and simulation, and so on.

Chandler (2002: 101) observes: 'While there are no opposites in "nature", the binary oppositions we employ in cultural practices help us to generate order out of the dynamic complexity of experience.' Binary oppositions introduce dichotomies into descriptions of change, dividing aspects of experience into antithetical groups. They are constructed out of negative associations between disparate ideas: the digital computer and the atom bomb become linked by being both antithetical to the idea of culture, the idea of progress or the idea of nature, rather than through any positive association arising from their shared characteristics.[1] Chandler (ibid.: 110) notes that 'opposites are rarely equally weighted'. Binaries of this kind are not just ways of carving up the world, but also ways of attributing value to different aspects of experience.

This function of linguistic binaries has been the subject of many semiotic studies. Lévi-Strauss's (1966, 1968, 1969) analysis of myth revealed how linguistic opposites contribute to moral frameworks, detailing the cultural function of different word-pairs: high and low; light and dark; and famously the raw and the cooked. Jakobson developed the concept of linguistic markedness, which expresses the idea that one term in any binary pair represents a norm from which the other is a transgression (Chandler, 2002). In each of the binary oppositions constructed within narratives of culture and technology, one term represents a valorised form that reinforces the cultural norm, and the other a departure from that norm. The concepts of 'real', 'human' and 'experience' represent ideal forms from which the concept of 'artificial', 'non-human' and 'simulation' are transgressions. This tacit weighting smuggles into the discourse of culture, society and technology ethical values that mediate our apprehension of change. They create a mythic frame of reference, in Barthes's ([1957] 1972: 112) terms a 'second order semiological system'; sign and signified together become a sign whose signification transcends their literal application and ties the binary to moral values and codes. This second-order system of reference performs the ideological function of naturalisation (Chandler, 2002); it functions to make certain ideas seem both natural and incontestable.

It is possible to trace the effect of linguistic binaries within the discourse of culture and technology by exploring one pairing of particular interest: culture and technology. To hold these two concepts in opposition is to imply tacitly their distinctness. This is in turn to circumscribe both what counts as culture and what counts at technology; at the very least it is to maintain that technology is not a part of culture and vice versa. But it is not clear that the idea of technology can be separated from the idea of culture in this way. The referent of culture is a complex of meanings, values, relationships, idea systems and material forms that resists final definition. The opposition of technology and culture treats that referent as a unified object defined by that opposition and responsive to a simple description; whatever else it represents, culture's quality is that of being 'not technology'. This tacitly valorises certain cultural forms, values and meanings at the expense of others. The work of art is more explicitly 'not technology' than the computer game. The novel is more explicitly 'not technology' than the e-book. But all these different cultural forms rely on technologies of different kinds, many of which are now normalised such that their opposition to culture is no longer felt.

Similarly, when everything that counts as culture is stripped from the referent of *technology* we tend to be left with material mechanical *things* robbed of independent signification and value. While the idea of technology can be reduced to material things, such as steam presses and digital computers, it also encloses notions that are distinctly cultural in nature. The *Concise Oxford English Dictionary* (2006) supplies the following definition of technology:

> 1. The application of scientific knowledge for practical purposes; 2. machinery and equipment based on such knowledge; 3. the branch of knowledge concerned with applied sciences.

This highlights the cultural basis of the idea of technology. The digital computer is not just a material thing, but encodes human knowledge in its materiality, reflects human aspirations and becomes meaningful because people use it to fulfil certain needs or desires. It is an imprint of human culture just as vividly realised as *The Origin of Species.* Culture runs through technology like the letters in a stick of rock. The false opposition of culture and technology strips the *things* of technology of their socio-cultural meaning, transforming the computer into nothing more than a twisted heap of wire, silicone and plastic, devoid of intrinsic meaning and significance. Holding technology and culture in opposition suppresses the complicity of technology and culture, and enacts a deeply corrosive reification of technology and its alienation from culture. Technology becomes the marked form, a transgression from naturalised human values. It becomes everything that is antithetical to the idea of culture, a strange and corrupting force, the mark of hubris, immoral and sanitised, leeching the humanity of those who employ it. This is not to suggest that we can never talk of 'culture' and 'technology' as distinct concepts in certain contexts, but simply to recognise that when we talk of their relationship we are discussing significantly overlapping ideas.

Similar points can be made about the other kinds of binaries that are established in the narratives of culture and technology. The opposition of real and artificial constructs not only a distinction between overlapping kinds of experience, but also a valorisation of supposedly 'real' phenomena over supposedly 'artificial' phenomena. It is a distinction that belongs not to the world, but to the way in which we describe the world. The experience of *Second Life* is every bit as real as the experience of real life. We do not become avatars in employing them; the disembodied world of the simulated environment is not a disembodiment of ourselves. Conversely the virtual world of *Second Life* is in many ways just as artificial as the built urban environment or the managed agricultural countryside. To label one *real* and the other *artificial* is to perpetuate a referential fallacy; what makes them real and artificial is only our insistence on the distinction. Similarly, the opposition of progress and regression forces us to consider human history as a grand narrative unforgiving of complexity in the historical process and in human lives. Progress and regression are just ways of framing change, not final descriptions in their own right. The opposition of human and non-human constructs an alienation of certain kinds of human experience that become complicit in the degradation of the idea of humanity. The earphones of iPods are no more extensions to our bodies than ceremonial piercings. Prosthetic implants do not imply the piecemeal replacement of the human body with silicone and steel, but are analogous to any other kind of tool that facilitates human action. These binaries reveal suppressed anxieties about the nature of technological change, but they belong to our descriptions of culture and technology, and not to the world.

How we describe experience, then, also moulds experience. Narratives smuggle unarticulated values into the discourse of culture and society. The idea of cultural decline, for example, presupposes that levels of culture can be objectively measured, and those levels compared. Alienation presupposes a supposedly natural human condition, recalling Rousseau. Transgression presupposes a natural order or law. Through their association with the cultures in which they are employed, technologies become attributed with human values: agency, and ethical and moral efficacy. The computer itself becomes an agent of moral decline, surveillance or morphological transgression. Digital technologies become moral actors in their own right, in denial of the social contexts within which they are deployed. As a result, technology itself becomes more insidious, dangerous and amoral. At the same time the characteristics of technology are projected on to individuals, social groupings and culture. New technologies provide new ways of understanding and explaining our experiences. But this metaphorical force of technological innovation can also result in a conflation of technology with its effects, or with other aspects of experience. When Descartes sought to describe the nature of the human soul he resorted to the metaphor of the clockwork automata in vogue at that time:

> And as a clock, composed of wheels and counterweights, observes not the laws of nature when it is ill made, and points out the hours incorrectly, than when it satisfies the desire of the maker in every respect; so likewise if the body of man be considered as a kind of machine, so made up and composed of bones, nerves, muscles, veins, blood and skin, that although there were in it no mind, it would still exhibit the same motions which it at present manifests voluntarily. (Descartes, [1641] 1962: 98)

The qualities of the automata function as a metaphor for the human body, but through the force of that metaphor become conflated with the things they help describe. In seeking to describe the function of the mind, Thomas Hobbes drew on the recent development of mechanical calculating machines, writing:

> When a man *Reasoneth*, hee does nothing else but conceive a summe totall from *Addition* of parcels; or conceive a Remainder

> from *Subtractions* of one summe from another ... for REASON ... is nothing but Reckoning (Hobbes, [1651] 1994: 20)

Leibniz similarly believed that all human reasoning could be reduced to a logical arithmetic on the model of mechanical calculating machines.[2] Turing ([1950, 1951a, 1951b] 2004) argued that the mind works like a digital computer. But the mind cannot always be explained by an analogy with the latest technology. Gardner (1987: 44) noted wryly that 'the rigorous application of methods and models drawn from the computational realm has helped scientists to understand the ways in which human beings are not much like these prototypal computers'.

Technology can also become a metaphor for its own effects. McLuhan (1962) saw in the regularised nature of printing an analogue with the systemised nature of Enlightenment thought. Technology changed not only the structure of written works, but by extension the structure of human thought. Castells (2000, 2001, 2004) saw in the digital network an analogue with its social effects; the network society becomes a way of explaining and containing the influence of the internet on social structures and human communication. In Postman's *Technopoly* (1992) the qualities of machines become projected on to the cultures and societies that use them; success in the technopoly is contingent on becoming more machine-like. In the narratives explored here, the nature of technology is frequently conflated with its socio-cultural effects. Alienation is rooted in a projection of the qualities of technologies on to the experience of the people who use them. But the filtering of the telephone is not a suppression of our senses. The flickering image rendered by the film projector does not replace our total sensory experience of the cinema. These forms do not come to *replace* lived experience; they are embedded within it. Temporal and spatial narratives project the qualities of technologically mediated communication on to the physical world within which that communication takes place. Technology does not in any real sense compress space or stretch time; it changes only the speed of communication and the efficacy of agency over distance.

Our experience of change and our articulation of that experience are tightly bound. It is not always clear how far our descriptions of technology's agency reflect real social change and how far they reflect merely our manner of framing and articulating our experiences. It would be overstating the point to suggest that perhaps the only significant difference in the digital age is in our narratives, but this does highlight the difficulty of separating out experiences from their articulation. The manner in which narratives mediate our apprehension of change, the different mechanisms by which they transform experience into stories that follow only their own logic, force us to question the degree to which the descriptions pertain to real change rather than just the *appearance* of change.

Historicising culture and technology

To transform the relationship of technology and culture into narratives is 'to locate experience in time and place' (Bruner, 1986: 13). It is to transform experience into events that possess temporality, occur in sequence, are causally related and are attributed meaning. It is to fit our experience within linear narrative structures that are unforgiving of possibility, uncertainty and dissent. But this may equally be turned on its head. To historicise culture and technology, to try to shape and attribute meaning to the intractable play of their cause and effect, is also to transform our understanding into a form of narrative.

The role narratives play in mediating, framing and containing our experience of technology's agency in the transformation of culture and society highlights the difficulty of discussing change within its historical context. Williams (1981: 33) has written:

> Much actual sociology of culture presumes, in a way inevitably, the typical or dominant relations of the period with which it is concerned; it goes on to adduce detailed evidence of these. But it can then happen that these relationships become a norm from which other periods are interpreted, or even, by contrast, judged.

There is here a broader question about how we understand the nature of history in the discourse of culture and technology.[3] But of more importance within this discussion are the discrepancies that arise in the aspiration to historicise social and cultural change in the very moment of its occurrence.

Narratives of culture and technology tend to conflate two very different frameworks for structuring culture and experience. Culture in the moment of its experience encompasses a significantly complex set of concepts, incorporating a range of reference within the social system, from beliefs, idea systems and value systems to the material products of cultural processes. Whenever we treat lived culture as a significantly total concept, we do so to understand the relationship between its many facets. As a consequence culture defies final articulation, and is always more than we insist it to be. But when we consider the past, we access only what Williams (1961) termed the *documentary* culture invested in cultural objects, artefacts and writings. This documentary culture provides only a partial record of past experiences, values and beliefs. The lived 'culture' saturates our social lives, but the documentary culture leaves only a trace. By contrasting the lived experience with the traces of the past, we never quite compare like with like. Asymmetries abound both in the nature and qualities of the evidence out of which we construct accounts of socio-cultural change and in our understanding of the values and experiences of different ages. In the transposition of the complex web of lived culture on to the dead, static trace of documentary culture we superimpose two different kinds of explanatory framework: the synchronic mode of logico-scientific or rationalist analysis, and the diachronic mode of narratives (Bruner, 1986; Chandler, 2002). To historicise cultural change in the very moment of its experience is therefore always to construct a reductive narrative, a partial idea of culture that reflects only particular kinds of change.

This effect can draw us rapidly into the trap of historicism. Popper (1957) defined historicism as the tendency to see necessity in the historical process on the basis of underlying laws, patterns, rhythms and trends, and as a result to draw the false conclusion that predictions about future events are possible. Because narrative forms precede the experiences on which they are overlaid, they give the false impression that the pattern of social change is somehow inevitable, or directional. Historicism is a persistent theme in the sociology of culture and technology. It is clearly present in certain narrative types predicated on the continuous and accumulative effects of technology such as decline and emancipation. But historicism also emerges in the epochs that are central to many accounts of socio-cultural change. Marx ([1859] 1968) described the transitions between slavery, feudalism, capitalism and the completion of the historic project in the classless society. Postman (1992) distinguished between tool-using culture, technocracy and technopoly. Bell (1974) described the movement from pre-industrial society, through industrial society, to post-industrial society. These progressive epochs aspire to the serial synchronic analysis of change, contrasting snapshots of stable states in different ages. But that aspiration cannot be realised. The pre-industrial and post-industrial societies that Bell described, for example, cannot be fairly contrasted because one is lived, saturating experience and the other is dead, a fading trace of the past. The idea of the post-industrial society will always be more filled in because it is fully situated within its historical context and reflects the complex web of values and practices as they are lived. By contrast the pre-industrial society is ripped from history, detached from lived experience, a documentary trace that compresses the cultures of many generations into one total idea, dispensing entirely with the complexity of lived experience. Even though such accounts wear the guise of analytical studies, they are also kinds of narrative that impose linear, selective accounts of change on to the complex web of culture.

Mark Weiser (1991) has commented: 'The most profound technologies are those that disappear. They weave themselves into the fabric of everyday life until they are indistinguishable from it.' Much of the social change that follows in the wake of technological development becomes over time normalised, such that the technology no longer seems to represent something strange or alien. Our society is littered with normalised technologies: agriculture, architecture, roads, metallurgy and so on. Yet when we think about the change that arises from technology, we focus only on the change experienced in the present, the effects of which are apparent to us. In constructing narratives of culture and technology we tend to ignore the experience of innovations and change in the past, the fears, anxieties and struggles with which technological change has always been met. A striking example comes from Freud's *Civilization and Its Discontents.* In discussing both the benefits and drawbacks of technology, Freud ([1930] 2002: 32) writes:

> What is the good of the reduction of infant mortality if it forces us to practise extreme restraint in the procreation of children, with the result that on the whole we rear no more children that we did before hygiene became all important, but have imposed restraints on sexual life within marriage and probably worked against the benefits of natural selection?

The reduction of child mortality in the developed world no longer strikes us as something to be resented, because it has become normalised such that an expectation now pertains to the survival of children through infancy. When we measure the past by our current concerns, we tend to exclude those anxieties in the past that do not resonate with us. This again results in a tendency to create too neat a narrative of change. But the quote from Freud also illustrates something else about change and how we apprehend it. Certain aspects of technological development correct previous kinds of social and cultural change. The drawbacks of declining infant mortality identified by Freud have been addressed by other technological and scientific advances, principally improved contraception. Technological advances are also framed by human desires and aspirations and by human nature, and therefore are to a degree self-correcting. But these subsequent self-correcting changes themselves become the site of renewed social tension and anxiety, without any acknowledgement of the previous changes to which they responded. The see-saw of social change, always accompanied by voices of dissent, suggests that it is change itself with which we struggle, and not its particular manifestations.

Narratives and personal experience

Why do narrative forms play such an important role in the way that we explain the experience of technological change? One possible explanation is that narratives are a way of creating meaning out of the flux of experience, and therefore fundamental to how we insert ourselves into the historical moment of the social system. Giddens (1991: 14) suggests that 'each of us not only "has", but *lives* a biography reflexively organised in terms of flows of social and psychological information about possible ways of life'. He stresses the reflexive act in self-identity; the manner in which each of us constructs out of a negotiation between experience and self a biographical portrait that is *lived*, or which in other words is played out in our interactions within the social world. In a manner of speaking, we *play* at being versions of ourselves. Giddens (ibid.: 53) argues:

> Self-identity is not a distinctive trait, or even a collection of traits, possessed by the individual. It is *the self as reflexively understood by the person in terms or her or his biography.* Identity here still presupposes continuity across time and space, but self-identity is such continuity as interpreted reflexively by the subject.[4]

The continuity of self is not a real continuity, but constantly reconstructed in the lived moment as a means of assimilating lived experience. In other words, we are constantly rewriting our autobiographical self in the light of our behaviour and experience within the social world. Self-identity becomes a negotiation between our past and our present, a negotiation out of which the continuity of experience and self is constructed. But self-identity is not just a negotiation between our past and present, it is also a negotiation between the present possibilities in our lived experience. Giddens (ibid.: 55) argues that self-identity is as a consequence both fragile and robust:

> Fragile, because the biography the individual reflexively holds in mind is only one 'story' among many other potential stories that could be told about her development as self; robust, because a sense of self-identity is often securely enough held to weather major tensions or transactions in the social environment within which the person moves.

The reflexive biography is a way of closing down the possibilities of experience: the people we could have been; the paths that we could have taken through life; the events that could have been avoided; and the opportunities that were lost. It is a way of shutting out the overwhelming anxiety created by the possibilities of being. But in securing the continuity of experience, the reflexive biography tacitly acknowledges the possibilities that it seeks to destroy. It is as a consequence fragile, always on the brink of falsification. The uncertainty of experience always threatens to overwhelm the coherence and continuity that we impose upon it. Nevertheless, despite this apparent fragility, the reflexive biography is sufficiently robust to contain the uncertainties of lived experience. And this is in part because it is *reflexive*; constantly rewritten to accommodate changes to not only our sense of selves in the present, but also our present sense of ourselves in the past. The memory of experience is a way of accommodating the fragility imposed on self-identity by possibility.

Personal narratives are the stories that we tell about ourselves and about the world to accommodate our lived experience. They provide a way of understanding our apprehension of social reality because they pick their way through uncertainties by linking ideas, experience or knowledge about which we can feel confident. Morson (1994: 38–9) has written:

> Narrative structure therefore falsifies in several distinct but closely related ways. It violates the continuity of experience by imposing a beginning and an ending; it reduces the plurality of wills and purposes to a single pattern, it makes everything fit, whereas in life there are always loose ends; and it closes down time by conferring

> a spurious sense of inevitability of the sequence actually realized. The very possibility of possibility is ultimately eliminated.

By falsifying aspects of lived experience and closing down the possibilities suggested by our lives, personal narratives also come into conflict with that lived experience. Czarniawska (2004: 5) pointed out that 'we are never the sole authors of our own narratives'. We are not free to tell any kinds of stories about ourselves that we choose, but are locked into a negotiation within the social world.

The significance of the events that make up narratives derives from their ability to *explain* some aspect of experience or knowledge. Significance is therefore dependent on the particular stories we are telling. Personal narratives are not fixed and final, but dynamically constructed within an entire social context. But change in the present also implies a change to our understanding of and relationship with the past, and the possible future. When we are confronted with new experiences, conflicts emerge between the kinds of stories to which we adhere and the realities of the social situation. Change in the present therefore brings us into conflict with out autobiographical past, leading to forms of cognitive dissonance manifest in the anxieties that emerge in the discourse of culture and technology. The reduction of dissonance usually represents a compromise between the way in which we think about ourselves, our behaviour and the world and our place in it, and our interpretation of the experiences that give rise to it. As we encounter new ideas, new experiences and new knowledge, we tend not to change our outlook fundamentally, but rather incorporate the changes into our existing way of looking at the world. We cling on to our values in the face of change. We are therefore drawn to ways of containing and explaining the idea of change that reinforce our values and beliefs, setting them in opposition to experience. As a result, anxieties rooted in the conflict between our narratives and experience are projected on to reality. The anxieties of technological change become a means of reasserting the continuity of self-identity in the face of challenges posed by lived experience.

Lyotard (1984: xxiv) argued that the post-modern condition is characterised by an 'incredulity towards metanarratives'; the certainties of the past give way under the assault of technological change.[5] However, this book argues that experience in the face of change is better described as a conflict between narratives. This conflict encloses different kinds of tension: the discrepancy between the ways we understand the world and lived experience, between the values to which we adhere and the reality of social change, and between our lived experience and the shared narratives of discourse and culture. The conflict saturates lived experience and is not exclusive to the digital age, but with the sedimentation of lived experience into a documentary culture the conflict in the narrative of the past remains opaque. This book explores the transformation that has accompanied the rapid and widespread adoption of digital information technologies as a process which saturates the whole lived social reality, and which encapsulates a kind of struggle between our sense of selves and our social situation. That transformation is the synchronic flux in which the mythopoeic nature of culture is forged. Historical change is an essential part of that process, but historical change is always mediated through the values and prepossessions of the lived culture.

Notes

1. See also Tredinnick (2006), Chapter 6.
2. See Tredinnick (2006), Chapters 3 and 4.
3. There is not space to explore that issue in any great depth, other than to note that this book adopts a view of history that draws on post-modernist historiography influenced by Foucault (particularly 1972), Jenkins (1991) and White (1978); that is to say that history is not understood to be a recounting of objective events, but an uncovering of subjective interpretations governed very often by the application of power. See also Chapter 8.
4. The italics are Giddens's.
5. See Chapter 7. See also Tredinnick (2006), Chapter 8.

Part II
Digital information culture

Textuality

In *Orality and Literacy*, Walter Ong (1982: 3) argued that the media and communications technology of the twentieth century created a 'secondary orality'. The telephone, television and radio all resulted in a decline in the importance of writing in the transmission of knowledge and information. Participation in culture became less a matter of mastery over writing and more a matter of mastery over a new oral discourse. If this is the case, then the digital age can perhaps be understood as inaugurating a secondary literacy. As digital technologies become more central to culture, writing has reasserted itself as the dominant mode of knowledge and information transmission. Through e-mail, wikis, blogs, social networking and instant messaging, text is becoming integral to culture, work and social relationships. We put text to more and different uses than ever before, distorting it towards communicative ends in more inventive ways. But this re-emergence of writing has brought with it a challenge to the stability of textual artefacts. Text has become a more mutable and malleable medium, torn from the control of the printing houses and publishers. As we move towards a secondary literacy, so our assumptions about what text represents become less secure. This chapter explores the status of text in the digital age. It first examines how printing changed the values attributed to textual works, helping to stabilise their referential value, and then examines how digital technologies undermine that stability, bringing us to a new reconciliation of the idea of text in the digital age.[1]

Textuality prior to print

By the time that printing with movable type was introduced into Europe in the fifteenth century, the trade in books was well established; the subsequent proliferation of presses largely reflected an already robust literary culture (Steinberg, 1974; Keen, 1990). Initially printing supplemented existing literary production. But while its social impact was more muted than is often implied, slowly printing changed the values attributed to both textual works and the medium of writing. Mumford ([1947] 2007: 97) argued that 'printing broke the class monopoly of the written word, and it provided the common man with a means of gaining access to the culture of the world'. Brewer (1982: 24) held that printing carried 'the stabilising, individualising, internalising effects of writing even further'. Something like this view is widely articulated. Some writers have attributed to print the foundations of the Reformation and Enlightenment (particularly McLuhan, 1962, 1964); however, Elizabeth Eisenstein ([1983] 2007: 96) observed that 'those who seem to agree that momentous changes were entailed seem to stop short of telling us just what they were'. Harris (2001: 235) warns against overemphasising the importance of technology in the status of writing, criticising theorists who exaggerate the significance of a 'literacy revolution'. Similarly Burrow (1982: 123) argues that printing 'made less immediate difference than might be supposed' and that the coming of print may be said to have done no more than accelerate existing trends in the consumption of literature. This chapter will argue that the effect of printing was slighter than often claimed, but no less significant for it, resituating the ontological status of the textual work.

Prior to the advent of print, the use of writing in all social classes was already well established. Social and economic changes through the fourteenth century led to a rise in lay literacy, and it is estimated that between 30 and 50 per cent of the population of England could read to some degree.[2] The burgeoning demand for writing was met by an increase in the production of vernacular and lay literature of all kinds. Texts were generally supplied through a decentralised provision largely dependent on ecclesiastical, university and administrative scriptoriums, and on a small but vibrant book trade (Burrow, 1982). In addition, textual dissemination occurred through private social networks, particularly among the newly affluent mercantile classes, with individuals participating in copying texts for their own use and the use of others (cf. Clanchy, 1993; Duffy, 1992; Justice, 1996). Mumford ([1947] 2007: 92) argued that 'the very aesthetic excellence of the illuminators and illustrators served also to retard the process of copying and so limit the circulation of books'. There is some truth in this, but the archetypal illuminated manuscript was only one kind of text in use immediately prior to print; within private and administrative contexts the slow and regular monastic book-hand was giving way to the quicker and more efficient cursive script (Burrow, 1982). Innovations such as the *pecia* system, which allowed several scribes to copy from a single exemplar, led to something like early mass production (ibid.). Nevertheless, the nature of the manuscript tradition severely constrained the reproduction and dissemination of textual works.

The decentralised nature of the manuscript culture contributed to the proliferation of variant texts: individual works filtered through culture via hand-to-hand transmission, gradually transformed as they were copied and recopied innumerable times. As a consequence no two copies of an exemplar were ever quite identical. The proliferation of textual variants also resulted from the way in which texts were reproduced: scribes played an active role in the creation of each text, not mechanically duplicating exemplars, but compiling, improving, expanding, contracting, translating, commenting on and censoring textual works. There was no practical way to control either the uses to which a text might be put or the changes to which it might be subjected after it had been released to the world. This mutability of text was recognised by the writers of the late medieval age; Chaucer noted the 'gret diversite In Englissh and in writyng of oure tonge' (Chaucer, [c. 1382] 1988a: 1793–4) and chastises his scribe because 'so ofte adaye I mot thy werk renewe, It to correcte' (Chaucer, [c. 1385] 1988b: 5–6). Text was both a mutable and a malleable medium; writing implied neither finality nor closure, and mutability was an inescapable condition of the use and transmission of texts.

The comparative scarcity of texts within late medieval culture meant that writing was always contained by and encountered within the wider oral culture; individuals need not necessarily be able to read to participate in the use of writing.[3] Keen (1990: 224–5) commented that 'for every reader there was a potential circle, small or great, of listeners, on whom the written word, through his reading, could have an impact'; Justice (1996: 33) that 'the literacy of one family member could be a delegated literacy for the entire family'. Writings of all kinds filtered through culture via different forms of oral delivery, from the sermon to the minstrel song. The assimilation of texts into oral culture meant that the dividing line between literacy and illiteracy was hard to draw. Reading and writing were not preconditions of participation in literate culture; the uses of writing within late medieval culture transcended the division between *literatus* and *illiteratus*.[4] As a consequence, texts were denied performativity, and tended to enclose the idea of their own oral performance. Medieval records recalled the memory of agreements, relying on the acquiescence and agreement of a real or conventional audience to that memory (Clanchy, 1993). Their authority was derived from oral practices; they recalled the performative acts that secure agreements, but did not themselves perform those agreements. Similarly, vernacular literature tended to enclose the idea of its own performance, appealing to the presence of an assumed audience.[5] Text became a means of recording the performances of oral culture, authority invested not in the textual artefact itself, but in the performative acts it recorded and recalled. Literate and oral cultures were finely interwoven, each intervening in the uses of the other.

As a consequence textual artefacts tended to possess a strongly iconic status, drawing on the richly iconographic nature of medieval art and culture. The cultural meaning of the textual object was not necessarily invested in the semantic meaning of the text it contained; the object itself often became an icon of its own semantic content. In an age lacking universal literacy the iconic meaning of textual artefacts was more widely accessible, and became as a result more potent. Clanchy (1993) has detailed how written documents came to complement and eventually replace other iconic symbols of entitlements and transactions. In the process they assimilated iconic symbols of agreement and functioned in a similar way to recall the memory of transactions. Justice (1996) traced the importance of written records to the Peasants' Revolt of 1381. Writing became the focus of the revolt, suggesting its potency and significance across the social spectrum. In several episodes the rebels demanded documents they believed secured their rights; it is doubtful that they existed, but while the meaningful content they were believed to possess remains obscure, they were identified by their aesthetic characteristics (ibid.). For the rebels, the objects themselves signified the cultural meaning attributed to them; what was actually written was secondary to their iconic function. The iconic significance of textual objects depended in part on the kinds of writing they contained; the meaning of highly formalised works, such as title deeds and legal documents, was invested in their status as signifying objects rather than in their status as meaningful texts. Such documents were meaningful to the literate and illiterate alike, and became widely employed by all social classes (Duffy, 1992; Clanchy, 1993; Justice, 1996).

Within a still predominantly memorial oral culture, texts represented not the site of knowledge itself, but the site of the creation of memory. The material presence of textual objects was not a necessary precondition of their use. Carruthers's (1990) detailed study of medieval memorial practice has demonstrated how reading was regarded as a process of memorisation; textual works were structured to facilitate memorisation, their paratexts of glosses and illuminations helping to secure the text within memory. Because access to manuscripts was limited, memory provided a more flexible and reliable way of manipulating textual works, allowing entire texts and parts of different texts on a single theme to be recalled without consulting the material textual vehicle. Memory was behind many of the uses of text; composition, for example, was rooted in the manipulation of memorised writing, and became associated not with original expression but with the reuse, reiteration and reforming of existing ideas and authoritative texts. Recalling texts on a particular theme became an important part of the skill of rhetoric and a site of the creation of new meanings. Texts living in memory were the site of constant reinterpretation, and of the constant production of new meanings.

The role of memory in securing the authenticity of texts influenced how textual veracity was understood; texts were memorised at the level of their sentence and more importantly their sense, or the literal rendition and thematic rendition of the text (Carruthers, 1990). Because the sense of the text was generally more valued than its sentence, fidelity to an exemplar was often a matter of fidelity to its thematic argument rather than to the literal letter of its text. Authority was rooted in the wider oral culture and secured against memorial tradition. As a consequence, originality was not invested in the novelty of ideas or expression, but in the novel use of lessons drawn from authority. The idea of authorship was not so closely invested in the original creative act. St Bonaventure distinguished four ways of making a book:

> Sometimes a man writes others' words, adding nothing and changing nothing; and he is simply called a scribe [scriptor]. Sometimes a man writers others' words putting together passages which are not his own; and he is called a compiler [compilator]. Sometimes a man writes both others' words and his own, but with the others' words in prime place and his own added only for the purpose of clarification; and he is called not an author but a commentator [commentator]. Sometimes a man writes both his own words and others', but with his own in prime place and others' added only for purposes of confirmation; and he should be called an author [auctor]. (Cited by Burrow, 1982: 29–30; the words in square brackets are the original terms in medieval Latin.)

Of these, only the last reflects the modern notion of authorship, but even here originality of expression or composition is not demanded of the idea of an 'author'. Not only does the *auctor* also rely on the words of others, albeit not in prime place, but that pre-existing authority is essential to the confirmation of the new text, and becomes the site of its authority. The expressing of existing ideas in an original way was more valued that the expressing of original ideas.

The method of building up new texts out of pre-existing fragments, ideas and traditions defined the cultural value of writing in the manuscript age. The composition of new works became largely a matter of weaving together existing texts and adapting existing sources to suit the needs of particular contexts or uses. This created a richly allusive textual culture, where the meaning of the individual work was situated not merely in its own semantic content, but in the dialogue it created with both other texts and the wider memorial tradition. Burrow (1982: 34) observes that:

> In this great age of the manuscript book, conditions encouraged a certain 'intertextuality' or interdependence of texts. Few works have the free-standing independence to which modern writers generally aspire; most are related to other texts by some degree of compilation, or translation, or even simple transcription.

The intertextuality of manuscript culture was enhanced by the use of glossing, literally the marginalia that explain and contextualise particular texts. Glosses tended to point out the sources of particular ideas and the relationships between texts. The authority of manuscripts was as a result not uniquely identified in the original authorial act, or with the scribal interventions that followed, but with the ideas to which the text alluded and on which it drew. Authority was not invested in the text as a manifestation of individualised expression, but in the text as an expression of the truths of memorial culture. Medieval textual culture lacked the individualising of authority that arises with print.[6] It was a participatory culture, in which individual works were transformed and recontextualised to suit particular needs. Texts were a site of the constant production of meaning, and every text became a kind of performance of the received truths of memorial culture.

The transition to print

Printing's most immediate impact was on the economics of literary production and consumption. The principal investment was shifted from the labour and time involved in copying and preparing materials to the initial costs of presses and fonts, and their preparation for the printing of individual works. Printing therefore afforded significant economies of scale as the marginal cost of reproducing individual works declined. Despite this, there was at first little significant impact on the volume of texts produced; print runs were initially small, ranging from about 250 to 1,000 copies per impression – similar to the scale of manuscript production in the late fourteenth century (Steinberg, 1974; Burrow, 1982). Manuscripts continued to be produced into the sixteenth century, and for a while the authority of printed works was distrusted by some (Duffy, 1992). However, over subsequent centuries there was a steady expansion in the volume of printed works, and printing became gradually more important to the cultural values associated with written works.

By centralising textual reproduction first around presses and later around publishers, printing helped to stabilise individual written works and the textual medium. Steinberg (1974: 20) argued that 'What was epoch-making in Gutenberg's process was the possibility of editing, sub-editing and correcting a text which was (at least in theory) identical in every copy.' The printed work was fixed and finalised before its dissemination; the point at which intervention in the text was possible was divorced from the text's reception and use, and centralised in the editorial and printing processes. Printing therefore contributed to the stabilising of individual works by reducing the textual variation found in manuscript culture.

A number of different elements of this increased standardisation are worth highlighting: material and formal characteristics of individual textual works, including script, page size, bindings and the materials on which works were reproduced;[7] paratextual frameworks within which individual texts were encountered, over time replacing glosses, illuminations and commentaries with title and content pages, and later indexes; variations in spelling and differences in English dialects, resulting in the loss of the *ash* (æ), *eth* (ð), *yogh* (ȝ) and *thorn* (þ) characteristic of English-language manuscript works, and eventually leading to the formalising of spelling and grammar;[8] and variations attributable to scribal error and intervention, which were replaced with printing errors and editorial intervention.

Printing not only helped stabilise individual works but also helped standardise the context of their discovery. Manuscripts were often prepared or compiled for specific purposes or readers, and tended to gather miscellaneous works within single volumes. An example is the Thornton manuscript (Lincoln Cathedral MS 91); probably compiled in the fifteenth century by the Yorkshireman Robert Thornton, it contains a miscellany of individual works, including romances, devotional items and a treatise on herbs and herbalism. This typical lack of thematic unity emphasises the way in which individual works in the manuscript tradition participate in a wider texture of literary culture by their often arbitrary juxtaposition. The particular context in which works were found became a part of the fabric of the work. Under the influence of printing, the kind of miscellany represented by the Thornton manuscript declined, leading to a greater thematic unity within published volumes. The reproduction of ostensibly identical copies of individual texts possessed of thematic unity helped fix, stabilise and standardise both individual works and the idea of the textual medium in which the cultural status of those works was invested.

As a result, the iconic status of the manuscript work drifted to an indexical association between the text and its formal characteristics. The sentence and sense of the manuscript text were united in the stable printed work. The *things* of texts became more significant than the external truths to which they alluded and which underpinned their cultural value. In particular, the characteristic qualities of the printed works became indices of their meaning and cultural value. Steinberg (1974) traced the increased standardisation of bibliographic information about printed works through the emergence of the colophon, and later the title page. These stable characteristics are reinforced through publishers' catalogues, library catalogues and the paratexts of printed editions. The particular qualities of texts that are valorised through bibliographic description centre on quasi-objective characteristics of text that impose certain conceptual frameworks which mediate understanding and interpretation. Bibliographic details presuppose an innate textual unity (Wolfreys, 1998) and act to direct interpretation (cf. Genette, 1997; Kristeva, 1980; Wolfreys, 1998). They presuppose the finality and closure of the textual work. They can be seen as mechanisms for stabilising meaning, and for asserting the possibility of the finalised text. But these are stable characteristics of *printed* works, and not of texts themselves.[9] They are therefore a way of imposing control over texts, and separating the textual work from the wider culture in which it is apprehended. While printing acted to stabilise individual textual works, reducing the drift to which they had been subject, it also acted to stabilise the textual medium within which they were reproduced, changing the value that was attributed to those textual works and making text itself seem a more stable vessel of knowledge.

This influenced the way in which texts were apprehended and understood within culture in a number of ways. In the first place, it destroyed the status of the individual work as a unique cultural artefact. Through its reproduction in multiple ostensibly identical copies, the printed text became merely a participant in an original authorial text rather than a unique cultural artefact in its own right. Its authority and authenticity were therefore not invested in its unique material presence, but in its participation in an original authorial act. Secondly, the availability of printed texts meant that their continued material presence came to be assumed. Texts lost their association with memorial practice, and this was reflected in the structure of printed texts themselves. Paratexts such as indexes, title pages and contents pages developed to help readers not to situate texts within memory but to orientate themselves within the material textual artefact. The presence of the textual object became a precondition of the uses of written works. Thirdly, texts became performative, but lost the allusion to their own performance. Documents ceased to recall the performance of agreements, and came to perform those agreements in their own right. This acted to sever literate and oral cultures; the printed text was not confronted and contained by the wider oral tradition, but abstracted from it. Its authority was not invested in memory, but in its own semantic meaning. Literacy became a precondition of access to and use of writing, and writing a more direct factor in social exclusion. Lastly, print acted to externalise the idea of knowledge, which became increasingly synonymous with the material vessels in which it was carried. The cultural meaning of manuscripts was always contained within the wider oral culture, and their semantic meaning created in the relationship between the reader and the text as it was integrated and incorporated into memory and memorial acts. By contrast, the printed text became a stable vessel for knowledge, separating the *known* from the *knower* in the process of knowledge transmission and aggregation.

But perhaps the most important shift inaugurated by printing was the valorisation of the individual authorial act. By eliding the role of the scribe, the reproduction of texts was transformed from a creative, inclusive and participatory act to a mechanical and exclusive act. An individual copy of a printed text was not a unique cultural artefact developed through the intercession of many hands, but participated in the idea of an original authorial text that it sought to reproduce faithfully and against which its authenticity was secured. Texts that had in the medieval period existed in a process of constant production became locked in a fixed final form. The author became the marker of the authenticity of the text, and originality became a more present expectation.[10] Originality was a quality against which the value of textual works could be measured, and was incorporated into the statutory framework through copyright law. This reinforced the idea of the text as a site of objective signification; the exegesis of medieval interpretation, in which layers of meaning unfold in the reading of a textual work, declined with the valorisation of a literal, semantic and objective meaning (cf. Robertson, 1962). Text became less a site of the constant cultural production of meanings, and more the site of a fixed, pre-given meaning deriving from the original creative act. Through its valorising of the individual creative act, printing isolated individual texts from their participation in a wider fabric of textuality; by the covers of the printed book were also severed the ties between works. The constant iteration of memorial truths that characterises what Burrow (1992) termed an 'intermittent culture' was replaced by the gradual accretion of knowledge in a 'continuous culture'.

Digital textuality

Printing's influence highlights how the mode of reproduction of textual works can affect the cultural values attributed to writing. It does not determine those cultural values, but creates a field of possibility for the creation, dissemination and use of textual works. By stabilising texts in the reproduction of multiple ostensibly identical works, printing contributed to the perceived stability to the textual medium itself. Writing was granted a uniquely privileged status as a stable vessel of knowledge transmission and the bedrock of cultural attainment. But in the digital age, both the stability of the textual artefact and the values that flow from it are less secure. Writing is becoming again a more mutable and malleable medium, under constant construction and devoid of final closure. The site of authority and authenticity in the digital texts is shifting away from the original authorial act and towards the digital text's participation in textual culture. This change in part reflects the different uses to which we put texts. Wikis, websites, blogs, e-mail, discussion forums, digital publishing, instant messaging, databases, newsgroups and RSS have transformed the use of writing, allowing collaboration in the creation of social texts, the endless recontextualising of textual works and a more playful treatment of the textual medium. But the change also reflects the mode of digital production and reproduction. The encoding, storage and transmission of digital texts make them intrinsically more mutable and malleable, allowing them to be used, disseminated and processed in a more flexible way.

In *The Meme Machine* (1999) Susan Blackmore distinguishes two modes of cultural reproduction: copying the instruction and copying the product. Manuscript and print reproduction generally functioned by copying the product; an exemplar becomes the basis of subsequent copies. They differed both in the fidelity of the copying process and in how fidelity was understood. For printed artefacts fidelity was measured against the original authorial text;[11] for manuscript works it was often measured against the ideas to which the text alluded. Digital texts are algorithmically produced at the point of consumption; their reproduction occurs through copying the instructions for recreating them during the cycle of transmission and use. Those instructions comprise different levels of encoding that distinguish qualities united in the materiality of printed and manuscript works. In the printed work, the structure, appearance and semantic content of the text are all united in the material object, a matter of the aesthetic impression made by that object. In the digital text, structure, appearance and content are generally independently encoded. The appearance of digital texts is as a result more mutable. Where printing acted to stabilise texts in the reproduction of ostensibly identical artefacts, digital technologies allow texts to be resituated within innumerable contexts where final appearance is often controlled at the point of display and not at the point of encoding, recording or transmission.[12] Unlike in the age of print, where the material object becomes identical to its encoded semantic content, resulting in an indexical relationship between form and meaning, in the digital age the apprehension of texts is unconditioned by their material form.

The digital mode of textual reproduction therefore results in the effective dematerialising of textual artefacts at the point of their consumption. Digital texts are of course contained in material vehicles of various kinds. However, the material base of digital texts is ephemeral, undergoing constant transformation during their use: pits on the surface of an optical disk, light in the optical drive, electrons within the computer, radio waves for transmission between devices and so on. Some of these constitute meaningful cultural objects in their own right, such as DVDs and CDs. However, while *culturally* meaningful, these artefacts are not *textually* meaningful; without their transformation through technological intervention their semantic content remains opaque.[13] In some forms the material vehicles of digital texts do not constitute meaningful cultural objects of any kind. It would be both difficult and meaningless to separate out the particular electrons that make up a digital text in the computer memory. The materiality of digital texts therefore has little impact on the way we apprehend them as meaningful textual artefacts. While the printed work is always tied to the page, the digital text is unconstrained by its material basis.

The effective dematerialisation of digital artefacts has a number of important consequences for our understanding of digital textuality. In the first case, because copying occurs at the level of encoding, virtually perfect fidelity reproduction becomes possible. Copying the product generally leads to progressive deterioration in the quality of duplication over successive generations; the copy of the copy is never quite as perfect as the copy of the original. But copying the instructions for recreating the product is less susceptible to this kind of deterioration. The copy of the copy becomes not only identical to the original, but undifferentiated from it. Secondly, the reproduction of digital texts incurs virtually zero marginal costs, and their transmission is virtually instantaneous. As a result digital texts undergo constant reproduction in the cycle of their use. When an e-book, e-journal or webpage is accessed, an impression of that text is created on the client device. When an e-mail is sent, a copy is created and transmitted. Although many of these copies are ephemeral, digital texts are nevertheless constantly proliferating, their traces etched on the media through which they are passed. Where print acted explicitly to separate the moments of reproduction and dissemination that in the manuscript age were often part of the same process of textual transmission, the digital age has reunited them again.

With the increased ease, cheapness and fidelity of duplication the economic barriers to the production of print-quality textual works have diminished. As a consequence the production of texts of different kinds has proliferated. E-mails, websites, wikis, blogs, social forums and newsgroups have all contributed to this explosion in the uses of texts. We now create more texts and put the medium of text to more varied use than at any other time in history. Informal social networks have also become more important to the creation, dissemination and use of text. Where printing acted to centralise the production in the printing house, and later in the publisher, and centralise the transmission of printed texts through booksellers and distributors, digital reproduction has decentralised both the production and the reproduction of textual works. Because digital texts are increasing disseminated by peer-to-peer transmission, intervention in the digital text is possible at any stage in its cycle of transmission and use. Whereas the printed work was finalised prior to distribution, the digital text is always open to subsequent intervention. Because only the instructions for recreating the textual object are copied, those interventions can occur without leaving a record or trace within the text itself. The digital text therefore lacks the finality and closure of printed texts. It remains alive to the possibility of silent change; the perfect copy may as well be a perfect forgery. As a consequence, the link between the copy and the original creative act secured through print reproduction is broken. Digital texts become the site of constant production and interpretation. The control over the final form of textual works exerted through the centralised publishing process is slowly withering.

The social text

The duplicability of digital text means that writing has become more integrated into everyday communication processes. Writing has been used as a medium for the communication of information over distance for many centuries; it was perhaps the earliest of communication technologies. But with the rise of discussion forums, SMS, instant messaging and e-mail, text has again replaced voice transmission as the dominant mode of interpersonal communication. The use of writing in asynchronous symmetrical communication has led to greater informality, and increased linguistic and orthographic drift. The Roman alphabet has been supplemented by a new range of typographical marks that help mediate communication, such as emoticons, a kind of iconic extension of punctuation. We have also seen the contraction of phrases in acronyms deployed within communicative contexts (e.g. LOL; AFAIK), which reaches its apotheosis in txtspk. The digital age has also spawned its own sociolect, leetspeak, or 1337 5p34k, which contains not only a playful typography, but consistent changes in word orthography and new word formations such as pwn3d (from a deliberate mistyping of 'owned') and n00b (newbie). These kinds of linguistic innovations have always been a part of the informal uses of text in letters, diaries and telegrams. But the digital text differs in also being the site of duplication and dissemination. These new uses of writing are both more public and more persistent than the informal writings of earlier ages. They share some of the characteristics of both the formally published and disseminated printed work and the informal private letter or telegram. These innovative and playful uses of writing are more than just personal codes and local language games, and become part of the living potential of the textual medium. This kind of orthographic drift undermines the cultural values invested in the idea of text as a stable vessel of knowledge codification and transmission. As writing is subject again to increasing change, the stability of the medium comes under question.

With the increasing use of writing as a medium of interpersonal communication, some digital texts are developing the markers of oral practices. Crystal (2001) has noted the way in which the uses of writing in certain digital contexts display the characteristics of both oral and literary practices, such as phatic utterance, whose function is to communicate presence and attentiveness in turn-taking exchanges. The increased use of asynchronous symmetrical communications contexts such as newsgroups, instant messaging and e-mail has also resulted in texts that allude to the idea of their own performance. This is a characteristic of the use of stage directions, a range of different types of which are evident: those which describe some gesture or action (e.g. *LOL* or *laughing out loud*); those that allude to a metaphorical gesture (e.g. *ROFL* or *rolling on the floor laughing*); and those that transform the textual space into an arena of performance. This last kind is the most interesting. Some online discussion becomes like plays, the medium of text containing both utterances and actions within an imaginary participatory space. Examples collected online include *passes boo a biscuit*, *pours a cup of tea* and *runs away crying*. These are transactional utterances that allude to metaphorical performances; their meaning is invested in the performative gesture and not in their textual description. These kinds of textual performances are not necessarily conducted solely for the benefit of the participants; in the context of online discussion awareness of a wider audience of *lurkers* – people who read discussion but do not contribute – conditions and informs many exchanges. The digital text is increasingly resituating texts within oral practices.

By passing through many hands in the cycle of their transmission and use, digital texts have become intrinsically less stable and more mutable. Texts and parts of texts are reused in constantly changing contexts. Blogs, mash-ups, websites and content aggregation all epitomise this process. As the text becomes the site of the appropriation of its meaning, the thematic and material unity of textual artefacts declines. This results in a kind of cultural *bricolage*, where new textual objects, such as blogs, are created from the recomposition of existing texts. Pieces of text become cultural actors in their own right. Certain kinds of texts become more clearly the product of many hands. This is explicit in the case of the wiki, where many people contribute to the creation of a single text, but it is also tacit in websites, blogs, social media and mash-ups. This represents a different kind of collaboration from that involved in the printed encyclopaedia or edited collection, both because the collaboration occurs at the level of the sentence of the text and because the text is subject to ongoing change. A Wikipedia article is not reducible to the individual writers who have contributed to that article; the article is not just an aggregate of individual contributions, but rather different contributions and contributors feed off each other, and the article becomes the site of an ongoing dialogue and negotiation.

As a result, the indexical association between the meaning and characteristics of texts of different kinds is destabilised. Texts that emerge through these new uses of writing do not have authors in the same sense as a printed text. They do not emerge in an original creative act against which the authority and authenticity of the work is secured, but emerge through the cycle of appropriation, intervention and reuse. This destabilises the authority invested in the original creative act; because the filiations of the digital text are more difficult to trace, the idea of the original creative act secured against a chain of duplication breaks down. As a consequence, the importance of originality of expression in textual works also comes under challenge. Plagiarism becomes more prevalent, perhaps not only because it is easier to copy the digital text, but also because its value is invested less in its association with an original author than in the ideas that it contains and to which it alludes.

Text and context

The proliferation of uses of text has changed the relationship between text and context, destabilising the indexical association between form and content of the printed work. In the manuscript culture, individual works were constantly reused within other contexts, both textual and oral, and collected together in new collections. Part of the meaning of manuscript works derived from the way in which they forged connections with other works in the wider textual culture. Paratexts such as glosses functioned to point out this innate intertextuality. With the increased formal unity of printed volumes, that rich intertextual field declined; individual works became severed from the wider textual culture. The meaning of individual printed works was invested less in the dialogue they created within literate culture, and more in their original semantic content. The paratexts of printed works changed to enable individuals to orientate themselves within the material artefact, rather than orientate the text within memory. In addition, the greater thematic unity of the printed artefact led to a correlation of the artefact itself with its meaning and content. This was reinforced through standardised bibliographic descriptions, where stable qualities were assigned to printed artefacts and standardised enumerated classification schemes sought to fit individual works within the whole structure of knowledge.[14] The emerging digital textuality undermines some of these effects of printing, returning us to the more intertextual field of manuscript culture.

The digital text is subject to constant decontextualisation and recontextualisation. The stable context imposed by the materiality and uniformity of printed artefacts is in decline. In the digital age the covers of printed journals have been ripped open as articles are increasingly encountered as unique digital objects. The bindings of books have been loosened, and individual chapters, pages and paragraphs reproduced independently of their context. Through the use of databases, texts are collected in ephemeral sets that respond to the particular search queries. Information retrieval systems construct temporary relationships between texts and parts of texts in response to individual needs. Web search engines reconstruct the entire visible ontological structure of the web in response to every search. Social software forges connections between texts on the basis of their popularity or user behaviour. As a result, in the digital age individual texts and parts of texts are more likely to be encountered as part of a wider textual field that transcends the limitations imposed by mechanical reproduction. Digital textual artefacts constantly find themselves rubbing side by side with different texts. They are no longer encountered through the imposed unity of their material presence, but have become more open to reuse, resituation and recontextualisation. Furthermore, because of the mutability of digital text, that intertextual field within which texts are encountered is itself more mutable, constantly changing as individual works are added, deleted and transformed.

The paratexts of writing have shifted to reflect the greater importance placed on context in the meaning of individual works. With the emergence of hypertext, the value of the textual artefact is reinvested in the dialogue that it creates with the wider intertextual field. Hypertexts borrow meaning from the other texts with which they are interlinked. The way in which individual texts and parts of texts are interlinked within a wider textual landscape means that they are never encountered in quite the same context twice; no two readings of a hypertext will be quite the same. By being subject to different contexts of discovery, the meaning of the text becomes both less secure and less closed, and more explicitly created in the act of reading rather than existing independently in the textual object. As hypertext has become complemented by hypermedia, textual objects create dialogues not only in an intertextual space, but also within a broader inter-medial cultural space. This results in a breaking down of the distinctions between the textual space and the wider cultural sphere that challenges the status of writing as the valorised medium of knowledge, literature and learning. The distinction between text, non-text and context is withering. The meanings of texts are shifted from their semantic content to the spaces between different cultural forms locked in a perpetual dialogue.

The unstable nature of digital text

The changes to digital textuality can be summarised as follows. As texts have become integrated into communications processes, they have taken on some of the characteristics of oral utterances, leading to a general orthographical drift. They have also become the site of performance. The proliferation of texts has led to a decline in the unity of the textual artefact; the stable printed vessels of texts that secured their unity have been torn apart. As a consequence digital texts find new meanings in the dialogues they create within their ephemeral contexts. The proliferation of texts has also led to a decline in the stability of the textual medium; because dissemination occurs through duplication, individual texts tend to be subject to more drift. Text is becoming again a more mutable and malleable medium. This unsettles the link between textual authority and the original creative act in which it is invested. As a result, the individualising of authority in the creative act and the mind of the author is perhaps in decline; texts are becoming a more social medium, subject to ongoing emendation to fit the purposes to which they are put. Digital texts therefore challenge the association between the authorial act and the authority of the text forged by printing, pluralising the notion of textual authority. As the stability of the printed text is replaced by the mutability of the digital text, the authenticity of the textual artefact can no longer be secured against its participation in an original creative act. Digital texts break the chain of duplication that printing erected to tie the text to its creation. They are less likely to be seen as a site of authority in their own right, and more as a site of the construction of meaning through social processes, an idea explored later in this book.

This destabilising of the cultural status of both the textual medium and individual textual works poses considerable challenges for how we negotiate cultural practices, norms and conventions in the digital age. With the emergence of a digital textuality the security of knowledge itself seems to come under threat, as the stable vessels of the past give way to a more mutable digital culture. The authenticity and authority of writing are undermined by the rise in informal publishing. The security of memory seems disturbed by a constantly changing textual record. In addition, the role of copyright regulation and plagiarism conventions buckles under the ongoing use and reuse of texts. But anxieties of this kind reflect a conflict of values in our apprehension of the textual artefact. We impose cultural values forged in an age of printing on to the digital artefact. This results in a confusion of the values of writing with the values of its mode of reproduction. We are troubled by texts that recycle and reuse other texts because printing has encouraged us to identify value with originality of thought and expression. We are troubled by texts that are composed from fragments because printing has encouraged us to identify value with compositional and thematic unity. We are troubled by texts that are constantly mutating because printing has encouraged us to identify value with the stable, fixed and finalised text. The allusion to performance contained in many digital texts undermines our association of writing and individualised, externalised authority.

These values emerged out of the mode of reproduction; they are not intrinsic to writing but are just one modality of writing. And while our values are still largely those of the printing tradition, digital textuality is not quite the same. Digital texts resist final signification and stability. They resist final classification and stable contextualisation. They are always straining at the edges of their own meaning. The incongruity between what we expect of textual works and how they assert themselves under conditions of digital reproduction creates a conflict of narratives in our approach to digital textuality. It is tempting to see in this conflict a return to something more like the medieval manuscript tradition. However, the apparent similarities between the cultural status of the medieval manuscript and that of the digital text arise simply from an undoing of the stabilising effects of printing. What emerges is a mode of textuality different from both the medieval and the modern, the possibilities of which are still to be realised. Just as the impact of printing on the cultural status of text was only slowly revealed, so the impact of digital information technology is likely to be both subtle and gradual.

Notes

1. This chapter focuses on the transition to print in the British Isles, although many of the issues discussed are equally relevant to the wider European tradition. For general histories relevant to this discussion see Clanchy (1993); Eisenstein (2005); Feather (1988); Fischer (1999, 2000, 2003); Justice (1996); Manguel (1996); McLuhan (1962, 1964); Steinberg (1974).
2. Levels of literacy in late medieval England are difficult to assess. For discussion of the issue see Brewer (1982); Keen (1990); Duffy (1992); Clanchy (1993); Justice (1996).
3. Derek Brewer (1982: 21) has called this intersection of oral and literate cultures 'one of the most interesting and important' aspects of late medieval literature.
4. Although difficult to draw, it was an important legal distinction. From around 1300, 'any person charged with a felony, who could read a prescribed verse from the Psalter, was theoretically entitled to benefit of clergy and hence escaped the death penalty' (Clanchy, 1993: 234). Clanchy notes that *literatus* and *clericus* came to be used interchangeably in the latter Middle Ages (ibid.: 226–30).
5. Burrow (1982: 53) has written that 'almost all Middle English writings betray the influence of "oral delivery"', but notes that 'the English writings of this period were not written exclusively for the ear'.
6. The name of no author of an English vernacular poem surviving from the twelfth century is known (Brewer, 1982: 24). Burrow (1982: 123) has observed that 'English Literature is in one sense a creation of the Tudor age' and that 'certain Middle English writers were incorporated into its canon and history posthumously'.
7. For the first hundred years printed works imitated the typefaces, layout and appearance of the manuscript tradition, generally employing the gothic script of late medieval manuscript works. Mumford ([1947] 2007) observed that 'it took a long time to discover that, to be an art in its own right, the machine need not, in fact *must not*, attempt to imitate the special graces of handicraft'. By 1501 the Italian humanist Aldus Manutius had not only introduced a range of pocket-sized books in octavo, but also employed the more readable and ink-efficient 'italic' font (Manguel, 1996: 137).
8. Although this was a slow process, still unresolved in the eighteenth century (Baugh and Cable, 1993).
9. For example, manuscript works do not have publishers, places of publication or years of publication, and often lack formal titles – the title may vary between different copies of a text. In addition, the idea of authorship was invested differently in the manuscript work, referring often to the textual authority behind the work.
10. The securing of the idea of authorship has come in for particular comment within post-structuralist theory. Foucault ([1991b] 1992) pointed out that the modern concept of the author is a post-Enlightenment creation. Barthes ([1968] 1977) argued that to give a text an author is to impose a limit on it, and attempt to provide it with a final signified value. Indeed, Foucault ([1991b] 1992) argues that the author really identifies an editorial function;

that it works to enclose texts, to enclose relationships between texts and to legitimise texts within discourse. The author is not intrinsic to the text, but imposed upon it in order to regularise discourse and knowledge. He argues that some discourses are endowed with an 'authorial function' while others are deprived of it, and that this distinction having changed over time maps the application of power within discourse.

11. The idea of the authorial text includes editorial interventions that may occur prior to its publication.
12. The degree of mutability in the final appearance of digital texts depends on the way in which they have been encoded. There are degrees of prescriptiveness of appearance in different file formats.
13. Cultural artefacts of this kind may have associated texts, such as the labels on a DVD, which become a part of the paratext of the textual artefact that they contain.
14. See Tredinnick (2006), Chapter 2.

5

Authenticity

This chapter explores the authenticity of cultural artefacts under the conditions of digital production, reproduction, transmission and dissemination. It will argue that in the digital age authentication and trust are no longer rooted in the material cultural artefact and its indexical association with an original creative act, but are constructed in the use of those artefacts within social contexts. Authenticity becomes what makes sense in the context of what is already known and already present. No longer tied to their point of origination or the manner of their creation, the authenticity of cultural objects rises up through the uses to which they are put. This chapter will use the terms 'cultural artefacts' and 'cultural objects' to refer to human-made artefacts with meaningful symbolic value, and 'digital' artefacts or objects to refer to both native digital cultural forms with meaningful symbolic value and digitised representation of material cultural artefacts.

The work of art in the age of digital reproduction

During the late 1930s the German cultural critic and sometime associate of the Frankfurt School, Walter Benjamin, studied the status of the work of art under the influence of mechanical reproduction. Although he regarded the cultural changes that printing had brought to be by then a 'familiar story', he argued that the consequences for the status of the work of art of different forms of mechanical reproduction, from lithography to photography, had only slowly become clear (Benjamin, [1936] 1970: 213). The cheapness, fidelity and volume of reproductions made possible by new technologies irrevocably changed the status of the work of art. However faithful, a reproduction would always differ from the original in 'its presence in time and space, its unique existence at the place where it happens to be' (ibid.: 214). While the value of the work of art was exhausted in its unique material form, the value of the reproduction was not. He wrote:

> This unique existence of the work of art determined the history to which it was subject throughout the time of its existence. This includes the changes which it may have suffered in physical condition over the years as well as the various changes in its ownership. The traces of the first can be revealed only by chemical or physical analysis which it is impossible to perform on a reproduction; changes of ownership are subject to a tradition which must be traced from the situation of the original. (Ibid.)

The work of art is distinguished from other kinds of cultural objects through its 'aura', which derives not only from the aesthetic impression it creates but also from its history as an aesthetic object, including its history of being regarded as of value. Benjamin (ibid.) argued that 'the presence of the original is a prerequisite to the concept of authenticity'; authenticity cannot function in the absence of that original. Mechanical reproduction severed the aesthetic qualities of the work from its material presence, and divorced the material history of the artwork from the contexts within which it is apprehended and discovered. Photography, lithography and film reproduced only a part of what contributed to the total impression made by the work of art; what could not be reproduced were its material history, its testimony and its context of discovery. Mechanical reproduction therefore replaced the unique material artefact with the generic copy, and in the process robbed both of their authenticity. This resulted in 'a tremendous shattering of tradition' that was 'the obverse of the contemporary crisis and renewal of mankind' (ibid.: 215).

But by freeing cultural objects from their materiality, mechanical reproduction also opened up the contexts within which culture could be discovered, encountered and used. Benjamin wrote:

> Above all, it enables the original to meet the beholder halfway, be it in the form of a photograph or a phonograph record. The cathedral leaves it locale to be received in the studio of a lover of art; the choral production, performed in an auditorium or in the open air, resounds in the drawing room. (ibid.: 214–15)

New technologies also created new cultural possibilities. Film and photography revealed the world in new ways: 'with close-up, space expands; with slow motion, movement is extended' (ibid.: 229). And mechanical reproduction created new conditions for the consumption of culture that produced 'a change in the mode of participation' (ibid.: 232).

Benjamin's work has been cited as the beginning of the post-modern mode of cultural critique, in which concepts such as 'authenticity' and 'authority' come under particular scrutiny (Malpas, 2005). It was widely influential on subsequent work on the influence of technology, particularly work in the post-modernist theoretical tradition. But Benjamin perhaps failed to recognise that the products of mechanical reproduction also derive authenticity in part from their material presence. The quality of the print or reproduction influences how we read it. The context of discovery of the reproduction also impinges on our understanding. A limited-edition numbered print is a unique cultural artefact in a similar way to an oil painting. The first edition of a printed work has its own kind of material value. Through the chain of duplication leading back to the site of creation, even in an age of mechanical reproduction authenticity remains invested in the original creative act. The importance of this continuing material presence is tacitly acknowledged in intellectual property legislation; the copyright of the material copy is said to be 'exhausted' in the individual copy, allowing the material artefact to live its own life. The restrictions on copying impose artificial limits on the scale of reproduction that continue to allow the work of art to participate in processes of ownership and control.

Many of the effects of mechanical reproduction can also be attributed to digital reproduction. Digital technologies extend the cheapness, fidelity and volume of reproduction of cultural objects. They strip the aesthetic object of its unique situation in time and space. But some effects of digital information technologies are different. Printing, lithography and photography replaced the unique cultural artefact with the mass-produced artefact, more easily manipulated and disseminated. However, digital technologies entirely strip cultural artefacts of their material presence, and in the process deny those artefacts their participation in the moment of their creation. This has an important impact on how we understand the idea of authenticity in the digital age.

Authentication and culture

In considering the impression created by cultural objects of different kinds, we can isolate five levels through which meaning is imparted. The most apparent and important of these is the aesthetic, semantic or symbolic form: the intentional or accidental meanings inscribed by the creator of a cultural object, or the meaningful impression on the audience that the cultural object aspires to create. This level of meaning is contained in the surface of cultural objects: the writing on the page encloses the semantic meaning of the article or the book; the compositional form of the work of art encloses its symbolic and aesthetic impression. When we talk of 'reading' cultural artefacts it is this surface level to which we generally refer. But it is not the only way in which cultural objects impart meaning. Second is the meaning that carries through the metacultural tradition within which cultural objects are situated; the way in which they both reflect and transgress the cultural traditions and circumstances within which they were created. The aesthetic character of medieval iconography or Impressionist painting ties them to the particular cultural environment that informed their creation. Third is the record or trace of the artefact's material history inscribed in its substance and form. The battered sleeve of an album and the dog-eared pages of a paperback both testify to their material history. Fourth is the context in which cultural objects are encountered or discovered. Cultural objects borrow meaning from their surroundings; the pile of bricks encountered on a building site has a different significance from the pile of bricks encountered in Tate Britain. Lastly is the knowledge that we bring to cultural objects: their history and significance; the traditions into which they fit; our preferences, beliefs and ideas; and our expectations. These different levels of meaning are not independent; each impinges on and directs every other. The idea of authenticity depends on the way in which these different kinds of meaning interact in the creation of the total impression of the cultural object or artwork. None of them survives unscathed through digital reproduction.

Aesthetics and tradition

Different cultural forms imply their own aesthetic possibilities and constraints – the possibilities of painting are different from those of digital art. From the aesthetics of cultural forms we can read two kinds of metacultural history: the history of aesthetic traditions, such as artistic or literary movements, and the history of technologies of cultural production. These two aspects are intermeshed but undetermined: the technologies of cultural production and reproduction constrain but do not determine the aesthetics of cultural products. The history of painting, for example, is tied to the history of pigmentation; because of their cost, blue and purple pigments in Renaissance art became signs of wealth. The authenticity of paintings can therefore be secured in part against the technical aspects of their composition. But pigmentation does not by itself determine aesthetic form. Similarly, the material and aesthetic qualities of printed works, including fonts and inks, change with the developing technology of printing; the aesthetic impression made by printed works therefore helps secure their authenticity. The aesthetic of newspaper production changed with the introduction of photo-lithography, and later web-offset printing and photo-composition. The constraints imposed by these conditions of production help authenticate newspapers as cultural objects. But in neither case do those conditions determine the aesthetic form of printed works. Different cultural forms fit into different metacultural traditions, but part of their authenticity always derives from how they both reflect and transgress those traditions.

Digital technologies create their own aesthetic possibilities. The previous chapter noted that while mechanical reproduction generally functions by duplicating the aesthetic qualities of the cultural product, digital reproduction generally functions by copying the instructions for creating the aesthetic qualities of the cultural product. Digital objects are algorithmically produced at the point of consumption; the reproduction of digital objects occurs through copying the instructions for creating them. At the point of consumption, digital objects are therefore often not fixed in the final form imposed on the products of mechanical reproduction. Digital technologies allow dynamic interactive modelling, enabling for example the real-time rendering of light sources and the manipulation of viewing perspectives to give an impression of depth and solidity. The experience of digital cultural objects is often more mutable, changing with the circumstances and contexts of each viewing. Part of the digital aesthetic is also a move towards hyper-realism: making objects look real without necessarily modelling real objects. The verisimilitude of the digital object therefore becomes an important component of its aesthetic possibility. Thus although there is some aesthetic loss in the digital object in comparison to other modes of reproduction, particularly texture, depth, solidity and material presence, digital technologies also offer new aesthetic possibilities. Platt (1995) has called the distinctive characteristics of digital rendering *immersion*, *rapture* and *agency*. Immersion is the sense of *being there*, rapture is the emotional attachment to digital environments and agency is the ability to assert control over digital objects. To this we can add discontinuity: the aesthetic or narrative experience of a film, book or piece of recorded music remains broadly the same with every use, but with a video game that aesthetic or narrative experience will always differ.

These qualities of the digital aesthetic impact on the idea of authenticity in a number of ways. In the first case they can act to detach digital artefacts from constraints imposed by the history of the technologies of cultural production. The authenticity of the film, for example, is drawn in part from its place in the history of cinema. Films both speak the vernacular of their time and are constrained by the technologies of production. The digitally remastered film overcomes the limitations of the technology of film at the time of its creation. The remastered *Star Wars* trilogy intervenes in the original print by recreating special effects shots and deleted scenes to retro-fit them into the style of the subsequent films.[1] Sound recordings draw their authenticity in part from the way they reflect the history of recording technology; the audio quality of Edison's phonograph cylinders testifies to their authenticity. But a digitally remastered sound recording overcomes the limitations of the recording technology available in the age in which it was originally created. As a result of interventions of this kind, the authenticity of the remastered film or album comes under question; it becomes difficult to distinguish the original creative act from subsequent interventions, and this poses questions about the degree to which digitally remastered works recover an authentic original work, and the degree to which they otherwise *invent* or *construct* an 'authentic' original that previously did not exist. Cultural objects are as a result increasingly severed from the metacultural traditions within which part of their meaning and value was invested.

With digital technologies we can bring back to life dead artists and actors, giving them new roles in film, television and music recordings. Natalie Cole's duet with her father on the re-recording of 'Unforgettable' (2000) relied on the digital transformation of Nat King Cole's voice. The Beatles re-formed 15 years after John Lennon's death to record the 'new' track 'Free as a Bird' (1995) from previously recorded demos. Similarly, Brandon Lee's continued starring role in *The Crow* (1994) after his tragic death was made possible by use of digital modelling. More recently, Elvis has been brought back from the dead to advertise BBC Radio 2 (*What an Amazing Line-Up*, 2006), and Bob Monkhouse has appeared beside his own grave to promote prostate cancer awareness (*Give a Few Bob*, 2007). Although with current technology this process relies on compositing existing performances, there seems to be no very good reason why in the future actors and musicians will not be reborn as fully rendered digital models. By copying the instructions for creating the performances of artists, rather than copying the product of those performances, we intervene in the constraints of previous cultural forms. This challenges the authenticity of both the composite forms and the original performances on which they draw.

The digital objects that result from this recomposition not only reconstruct the traditions they contain, but are also often detached from them. When the film can be remade, the actor reborn, the album remastered or the image digitally enhanced, each becomes semi-independent of the grammar, the dialect and the vernacular of the cultural traditions in which it was originally situated. As digital objects, the new forms become a part of the metacultural tradition of digital culture; the possibility of compositing performances becomes a part of the vernacular of the digital age. Yet despite this it is not merely the existence of new cultural forms of this kind that is of interest, but what their existence implies for both the continuity of the cultural tradition and the understanding of older cultural forms. This reuse of aspects of culture changes not only how we view the composite works that result, but also the originals from which they are derived. As a result of digital technologies, existing cultural artefacts are always open to being resituated in full or in part within new contexts. That resituation and recontextualising becomes a part of the vernacular not only of digital culture but of the culture of prior ages. Digital reproduction challenges the very idea of tradition. The uses of cultural forms, objects and performances transgress the limitations of the original creative act.

Materiality and context

Part of this undermining of the idea of tradition arises from the dematerialising effect of digital reproduction. The material presence of cultural objects provides clues to their meaning and value. The scale of works of art directs our interpretation of them, creating impressions of intimacy or grandeur, distance or involvement. The reach of a sculpture or building that seems to deny its own weight is part of the meaningful impression that it creates. Material clues that direct interpretation in this way are equally important to the products of mechanical reproduction. The quality of paper, printing and binding directs our apprehension of written works. The weight of a book in the hand is a part of the impression it gives; we talk of 'weighty books' and 'light reading' because of the link between the tactile and cognitive experiences of reading. The gatefold album sleeve or box-set DVD collection becomes a part of the meaningful impression these objects make on us, influencing how we understand their contents. In these examples, the material and the aesthetic combine to give a total impression of the cultural object. But digital artefacts are unconstrained by their material form. At the level of their cultural meaning they do not possess substance, weight, volume or texture; there is no such thing as a weighty e-book, a gatefold download album or a streamed video box-set. In addition, technologies for the display of digital objects tend to lead to their homogenisation and flattening. The material clues to the scale of the cultural work are stripped from the digital reproduction. Paintings of different proportions occupy the same digital space. Digital technologies therefore undermine the connection between materiality and form, and tend to homogenise cultural objects.

The materiality of a cultural object inscribes a record or trace of its history. From the surface of a painting we can read both the process of composition and the material history of the object itself. Similarly, when we look at a book we can read from the page not only the text itself, but also the history of that text, the marks of prior readings, the broken spine, the marginalia or the folded corners of the page. The deterioration of celluloid is projected on to the cinema screen, and photographs deteriorate and fade with time. These material markers of age and use become a part of the meaning and value of the cultural object, securing its authenticity through the correlation between expectation and actuality; we expect old works to bear the scars of their age. Material markers of this kind tie us to the point of creation: to the hands of the artist or to the chain of duplication reaching back to the original creative act. As a consequence of the continued investment of authenticity in the original creative act, the antique print and the first-edition book become more valued because they are objectively closer to the moment of creation. Even with mechanical reproduction the point of origin continues to secure authenticity; age and authenticity often become conflated.

While a DVD is a cultural object in its own right, the digitised painting stored on it is not tied to the materiality of the DVD in the way that the original is tied to its canvas and paint. Intervention in the digital object can occur without leaving a trace in its material vehicle. Over-painting in a digital work of art is virtual and not material; it replaces rather than supplements what was previously inscribed. Digital remastering of a film or album and digital retouching of a photograph leave only aesthetic and not material traces. The ease of intervention in the digital artefact, and the lack of the trace of that intervention, mean that the authenticity of the digital object is difficult to secure against its material testimony.

Furthermore, although the media of storage may degrade over time, digital artefacts generally remain unchanged. A DVD will deteriorate, but if migrated between media the digital image will not itself decay. Because digital artefacts do not deteriorate they cannot be authenticated against the trace of their material history. Digital artefacts do not exhibit the scars, marks and traces of use. They do not age. They do not fade. Digital artefacts are therefore severed from the material history of their use, floating free of the material world. And this changes what we expect of other kinds of cultural artefacts; the perfect copy creates an expectation of a perfect artefact. The deterioration to which traditional cultural objects are always subject becomes a marker of a new kind of inauthenticity demarcated by the shabbiness of the real.

Finally, the material presence of the cultural object secures its status in part by limiting access and use. Even under conditions of mechanical reproduction, copyright and intellectual property rights secure the scarcity of cultural forms. But digital artefacts constantly migrate between different material vehicles in the process of creation, dissemination and use. No one material form is intrinsic to their nature. This results in near cost-free duplication with near perfect fidelity.[2] The hundredth-generation copy of the digitised painting will not differ significantly from the original digital image. The copy and the original in many ways become indistinguishable. This perfect fidelity duplication destabilises the filiations of duplication that tie both the mass-produced cultural object and the unique cultural artefact back to their point of creation. Whereas the products of mechanical reproduction are authenticated against the publisher or producer, tying them back to a point of origin, the products of digital reproduction tend to filter through culture via informal and ephemeral social networks. Digital reproduction breaks the chain of copying by which authenticity is handed down through mechanical reproduction of an original exemplar, in which copies borrow the authenticity invested in the original creative act. Under these conditions, cultural objects are unconstrained and unleashed.

It has been noted that cultural objects borrow meaning from the contexts within which they are encountered. The urinal of Marcel Duchamp's *Fountain* and unmade bed of Tracey Emin's *My Bed* both mean something very different when isolated in the gallery than in their original environments. A painting in a national collection is apprehended differently from a painting in a commercial gallery. Da Vinci's 'Last Supper' is inseparable from its context, painted on to the fabric of the refectory in the convent of Santa Maria delle Grazie and integrated into its architectural space. These contexts are part of the material history of the cultural object: the unique status of the work of art secures its presence in one place. Context is also important to the products of mechanical reproduction. The presence of an article in a particular journal, or in a particular issue, will change the way we read it depending on the dialogue that it creates with the other articles with which it is collected. Television programmes borrow audiences from the programmes that precede or follow them. The single borrows significance from the other songs on an album. Different ways of carving up objects of culture lead to different kinds of impression: the mix tape is different from the artist's album; the same image contained in a picture calendar and gallery catalogue will have different connotations.

Like mechanical reproduction, digital information technologies tear cultural objects from their original contexts. 'The Last Supper' has been wrenched from the plaster of the convent of Santa Maria delle Grazie. Stained-glass windows are ripped from the cathedrals that frame their meaning. The aesthetic form of illuminated manuscripts is ripped from the vellum and reproduced on the screen. But the mode of digital reproduction also results in the recontexualisation of digital objects in innumerable new surroundings. Unlike in the age of mechanical reproduction, digital appropriation and recontextualisation of cultural objects proliferate in every use of digital technology. The site of reproduction is not limited to the owners of the means of mechanical reproduction, but subsists in the use of digital technologies. The appropriation and recontextualisation of digital objects do not occur prior to the point of their reproduction, but at or near to the point of their consumption. Digital objects are therefore more integrated into the contexts of their use, and the contexts within which value and meaning are attributed to them.

Cultural granularity and *bricolage*

We can now begin to trace the outline of digital culture. One of the effects of digital technology is the decontextualisation and recontextualisation of cultural forms, objects and traditions. This changes how we view not only the new digital objects that result, but also the originals with which they participate and from which they draw part of their meaning. As cultural objects are introduced into new contexts, the meaningful value of the original works also shifts. This is not just a factor in the digital culture, but integral to the way in which cultural objects, ideas, forms and performances are perpetuated and received. For example, the use of Puccini's 'Nessun Dorma' in the coverage of the 1990 World Cup meant that for millions of people the song became associated with football. Dan Brown's appropriation of 'The Last Supper' in *The Da Vinci Code* (2004) means that for his millions of readers the painting has become associated with a particular narrative. The artefacts of culture have always been subject to this cycle of appropriation and reuse, a cycle that creates a dialogue between existing cultural forms and the emerging products of culture. Cultural creativity can perhaps be understood as the forging of this dialogue with tradition. However, while the use of cultural forms, traditions, performances and artefacts has always implied a cycle of appropriation and reuse, the digital age differs in the site of that appropriation. The reproduction of cultural objects has shifted closer to the site of their consumption, and this has meant that we are all more complicit in the creation of a peculiarly digital culture.

In the age of mechanical reproduction, the meaningful unit of culture tended to be tied to the single cultural object: the painting; the work of literature; the piece of music. Technologies of mass reproduction tended to reinforce the integrity and unity of these cultural objects through the unity of the reproduced artefact. The book, the album and the film are pre-packaged units of culture that fit the needs of a marketplace. But in the digital age, the meaningful unit of culture is no longer limited to what can be meaningfully inscribed in material vehicles. Aspects of larger works can be ripped, mixed and recontexualised in different contexts in a more active, open and accessible way. The fragment of the painting is wrenched from the canvas and takes on a recontextualised meaning in the new environments within which it is reproduced. The single is torn from the album and sold as a download or ring tone. The sample is ripped from the single and used to create new music. The actor is cut out of the scene, and his or her performance recomposited in an entirely new film. Part of the effect of digital reproduction is the tendency towards the fragmentation of cultural forms and destruction of their continuity, integrity and consistency. And this is not just a matter of the intertextual allusion within the product of culture to other works, but the incorporation of elements of those works within the new cultural artefact.

Culture has become as a result more atomised and granular. The effect is a kind of cultural *bricolage*, in which new cultural forms are constructed out of the detritus of the old. Under these conditions, the value and authenticity of cultural objects are reinvested in a participatory mode of cultural production. Mechanical reproduction tended to contribute to the separation of the cultural artefact's moment of creation from its moment of consumption. By contrast, digital technologies have tended to bring those moments together. As new media technologies place the power of media producers into the hands of consumers, the dividing line between creators and audiences is blurring. A more participatory cultural field is emerging in which increasingly cultural objects become either composites and collages or are playfully constructed out of allusions to the wider cultural field. This participatory mode of culture takes place both within existing frameworks of production, ownership and control and beyond them. Television producers draw on user-generated content to fill out their schedules and expand the involvement of the viewer, and newspapers have extended the involvement of readers beyond the letters page to online discussion forums and blogs. At the same time, we have seen the growth of different kinds of cultural artefact that create a dialogue with existing cultural forms, such as fan fiction and fan films.

Increasingly, digital environments and social networking services are allowing audiences to participate in the creation of media and culture independently of traditional media organisations. Blogs allow people to recontextualise and comment on the news that they think worth reporting. Video networking sites have allowed users to create and contribute their own video content. Wikis allow users to contribute to the creation of shared distributed texts. Documentaries like *Loose Change* (2006) compete with global media outlets in terms of their reach and influence. In each of these cases, digital technologies are shifting the value of the cultural artefact from the material object to the process of participation. The objects of culture are no longer secured behind glass cases, tied to the walls of museums and galleries or constrained by the control over publishing and broadcasting, but are created and recreated in the social process.

Jenkins ([2003] 2006) argues that 'patterns of media consumption have been profoundly altered by a succession of new media technologies which enable average citizens to participate in the archiving, annotation, appropriation, transformation and recirculation of media content'. Web-propagated fan fiction allows readers to participate in rewriting and extending works of literature. The results are of variable quality and taste, but in them the work of fiction lives beyond the confines of the page, reinvented and reimagined in the minds of its readers. The genre of slash fiction, in which the characters of literature or film become the protagonists in unlikely sexual encounters, exemplifies this playful engagement with the boundaries of cultural forms.[3] The play of slash fiction is invested in challenging the conventions of dramatic and literary narratives. A similar kind of play with existing cultural forms occurs in amateur film-making. Student and hobbyist productions such as *George Lucas in Love* (1999), *Trooper Clerks* (1998) and *The Jedi Who Loved Me* (2000) play with and extend the Hollywood films on which they draw and with which they create a dialogue (Jenkins, [2003] 2006). *George Lucas in Love*, for example, merges the narratives of *Shakespeare in Love* (1998) and *Star Wars* (1977), portraying Lucas as a film student struggling with writer's block, surrounded on his campus by characters and situations that echo those in his films. More recently, the simulated environments of computer games and immersive social worlds have been used to create short films; the models and environments of games lend themselves to dramatic narratives, although the result is sometimes incongruous. Many of the creators of amateur films are drenched in movie culture, playing with allusions to commercial releases in their work. Many also aspire to careers in commercial film production, and use amateur films to perfect their craft or publicise their skills (Jenkins, [2003] 2006). Over the last few years YouTube has provided an outlet for many of these films, but YouTube did not create the kind of *bricolage* play they exemplify.

One consequence of this cultural *bricolage* is an assault on traditional notions of ownership, copyright, plagiarism and fair use. Jenkins ([2003] 2006) noted that fans involved in film-making reject both the idea of a definitive, produced and authorised version of a film and the intellectual property control of media conglomerates:

> Instead they embrace an understanding of intellectual property as 'shareware', something that accrues value as it moves across different contexts, gets retold in various ways, attracts multiple audiences, and opens itself up to a proliferation of alternative meanings.

This has sometimes brought amateur film-making into conflict with traditional movie producers. Fan fiction and slash fiction have similarly often come into conflict with publishers keen to maintain control over the representations of fictional characters. Some of the companies most associated with perpetuating participatory culture, such as YouTube and Google, steer a fine line between fair use and copyright infringement. This tendency for digital technologies to undermine control over intellectual property has brought with it anxieties about the future of creativity and culture.

Within the anxiety about a loss of control over the products of creative effort lies a conflict of values, and two distinct accounts of where the meaning and worth of cultural artefacts lie. Copyright is underpinned by the creative act involved in a literary or artistic work – an act not necessarily of an individual, but an act that secures the origination of a new creative work from which all subsequent rights follow. It is also underpinned by the unity of the work, such that the work is to be taken as a whole, and exploitation of part of that work is referenced to this whole. Copyright emerged with and mirrors the structural qualities of mechanical reproduction, where duplication results in ostensibly identical copies. With mechanical reproduction, meaning and value become invested in the original creative act and in the intention of the author or artist. Copyright is therefore not intrinsic to cultural objects and their reproduction, but is imposed upon them by legal and regulatory frameworks as a means of regulating their exploitation.

Underpinning the challenge to copyright posed by digital technologies is a cultural shift in the basis on which meaning and value are invested in cultural objects within participatory culture. The digital age is witnessing the death of the cult of the individual, in which authenticity is tied to an original creative act and secured against the identity of the creator. The mutability of digital information and collaborative approaches such as wikis, discussion groups and the open source movement problematise the value invested in that original creative act. The *bricolage* culture is by its nature reconstituted out of existing cultural forms, from fiction, film and newspaper articles to computer games and art; meaning is invested not in the final artefact but in the dialogue that it creates through its use, recontextualisation and reincorporation into the cultural field. The ease, cheapness and fidelity of the digital copy mean that digital objects are always subject to endless duplication and proliferation. The shift in the point of duplication closer to the point of consumption means that digital objects are always subject to interventions that change their structure, form and meaning. The greater role of social networks in the distribution and dissemination of cultural artefacts undermines the control of the printing house, publisher or distributor. New digital technologies, from the web to peer-to-peer networking services, always threaten to undermine control over intellectual property rights.

Digital authenticity

By destabilising cultural objects and their authentication, digital technologies undermine the ways in which meaning is created and imparted by the artefacts of culture. The value and meaning of individual objects are disinvested from their intrinsic material and aesthetic qualities and reinvested in their contextual use. Artefacts and their meaning or value become partially divorced. With the declining importance of material presence in our apprehension of the cultural world, the authenticity secured against the presence of physical things itself declines. The value of cultural objects becomes no longer unanimous with and identical to their own history, testimony and contexts of discovery. Digital technologies therefore seem to imply a total and irrecoverable loss of the idea of authenticity; a loss of the ties that mechanical reproduction maintained with the point of origin, against which rights are secured and value measured. With the impossibility of tracing origin and intervention, the digital age appears to be a culture without reverence, stripped of value, beholden to the passing image, enamoured with the surface patina but uprooted from tradition and barren.

However, digital artefacts gain authenticity in new ways unlinked to their material status. Their authenticity derives not from their participation in an original creative act secured in the material artefact through the chain of duplication, but from their being actively and continually valued, used and held credible. Individual images, photographs or films gain authenticity by being widely reproduced through social networks. Individual articles gain authenticity by being repeatedly blogged or interlinked within a wider textual culture. They borrow authenticity from the judgements of their users in their being held as significant, serious or exemplary. The whole cultural field of digital communication becomes a filter of developing values, traditions and beliefs. In addition, authenticity is stripped from the object as a culture actor in its own right, and reinvested in the forms from which it is composed and composited. We recognise the fragments of images, paintings, performances and music ripped from their original contexts. This reuse of the cultural *bricolage* directs our attention back to the sources of the borrowing. Cultural objects of this kind create a kind of dialogue between themselves and the forms on which they draw. They perpetrate an infinite deferment of meaning through webs of allusion and signification. The objects of culture become self-referential, playfully acknowledging their own artifice. Any investment of authenticity in the creative act is transformed into a culture of discourses, of reuse and recontextualisation. Digital culture itself becomes like Herman Hesse's *Glass Bead Game* ([1943] 2000), the abstract synthesis of knowledge, art and tradition played out in the connections forged between seemingly unrelated cultural forms.

The dynamic nature of the authenticity of digital artefacts challenges many of the assumptions about knowledge, information and culture that we have adopted from previous ages. Through its objectification in the material artefact, the work of literature becomes something that sits on the shelf, largely independent of the reader and outside of social processes in which it plays a role. The meaning and value of the book become a quality of the object itself as much as of the way in which it is read, secured against the original authorial act and intention. Through its objectification in the material artefact, the work of art becomes something that sits on the wall independent of the viewer and outside the process of being apprehended. It becomes something that can be described in publishers' catalogues and classified among artistic movements. The meaning and value of the work of art become a quality of the object itself as much as of the way that it is viewed, secured against the creative act and the artistic intention. Through its objectification in the celluloid reel, the film becomes a finalised and finished product, its meaning and value invested in its stable material form as much as in the way that it is watched. In each case the cultural object is already a *fait accompli* prior to its incorporation into lived culture, closed, finalised, petrified and static. Cultural forms that were once rooted in social practices, such as the painting on the cathedral wall or the stained-glass window, and once a part of the lived culture, become abstracted, preformed and silenced.

But through digital technologies, this objectification of culture is undone. Forms, practices and traditions are reintegrated into the lived social processes through which they are created, used and valued. The work of art becomes a more present part of the lived culture, not just for those who file past it in reverential silence in the art gallery, but also for everybody else beyond the gallery walls as it is disseminated across the social network. This is not merely a matter of opening up access to the work of art, but of opening up the work of art itself, allowing it to carry multifarious meanings in different contexts of use. As a consequence the meaning of cultural objects becomes less given, imposed and controlled by the contexts in which they are allowed to be discovered, and becomes more active, created in the lived moment of their consumption. Meaning is more actively created within the whole social process, transforming the cultural sphere from a static collection of objects, forms and performances to which we can merely add, our participation always deferred, into a field of *play* in which the value of everything is open to negotiation.

It is dangerous to overemphasise the significance of the dematerialisation of cultural objects; most of our life is still lived in the material world. Nevertheless the digital age does create this new field of play in which the documentary culture of artefacts is perhaps being reintegrated into the lived culture of our whole way of life. By doing so it also challenges some of the assumptions that developed about the status, meaning and value of different cultural forms, practices, traditions and performances when the proliferation of dissemination of a documentary culture was filtered through limited channels. This forces us to rethink not only the value that we attribute to digital culture, but also the value we attribute to those documentary traditions, practices and forms that it threatens to undermine. This is not an objective change to the nature of the work of art, literature, film or music; creativity survives different modes of its expression. Instead it is merely a change in how we slot the artefacts of culture into our narratives of the social world.

Notes

1. For example, in a deleted scene from the first film, the character of Jabba the Hut was played on screen by an actor. When the original deleted scene was reincorporated into the digitally remastered film, a CGI image was inserted into the scene to replace the actor, ensuring continuity with the sequels.
2. In fact there is some degradation in the copying process, but the error rate is very small.
3. The 'slash' of slash fiction refers to the '/' mark separating character names out of which the titles are formed, e.g. *Kirk/Spock*.

6

Knowledge

This chapter explores notions of truth and knowledge in the digital age. It argues that we are moving away from an individualising objectivist view of truth and knowledge, secured against the authenticity invested in cultural objects themselves, towards a pragmatic constructivist idea of knowledge creation and transmission. It was noted in previous chapters that the dematerialising of cultural objects and texts leads to a stripping away of authenticity and its reinvestment in the processes of creation, dissemination and use. This reinvestment of authenticity in the social process has resulted in a diffusion and proliferation of truths, leading to what some theorists identify as a post-modern cultural mode where all truths become equal. But this chapter will argue not that the security of knowledge is undermined by digital technologies, but rather that the cultural mode through which knowledge is authorised is laid bare by the growing visibility of competing truth claims. The digital age does not shatter traditional notions of trust and authority, but exposes them for the socially situated and culturally constructed processes that they always were.

Fractured truths and declining authority

The digital age seems like an era that has lost both faith in objective truths and trust in traditional sites of authority. The shared value systems and social structures of the past seem to be in terminal decline. Some concrete examples drawn from the UK are worth highlighting. Affiliation and identification with the major Christian denominations have been in decline for about 40 years. In 1964 three-quarters of the population claimed to belong to a religious group and attend services; by 2005 that number had fallen to under a third (Heath et al., 2007). Over the same period the proportion of people claiming no particular religious affiliation rose from 3 per cent to 38 per cent (ibid.). Perhaps the starkest indication of declining religiosity comes from the 2001 Census returns, where almost 400,000 individuals recorded their religion as 'Jedi' (ONS, 2003). The decline of religiosity appears to reflect not only a fall in participation but also the weakening role of religious beliefs in social identity (Heath et al., 2007). This has disproportionately affected the established Anglican Church; while only a third of Anglicans believe they have a lot or a little more in common with other members of their faith group, for non-Christian faiths that proportion is over 80 per cent (ibid.). While participation in and identification with the major Christian denominations have declined, some smaller religious groups have grown: new-age spiritualism, paganism and other secular forms of religiosity have found their membership figures swell. In 1999 the BBC reported that there were over 100,000 practising pagans, 20 times the number a decade previously. This rise of smaller denominations and alternative faiths is not sufficient to make up for the decline of established Christianity, but highlights how in matters of faith individuals are increasingly turning away from the traditional sites of authority and towards more personal truths.

Like religious affiliation, membership of political parties and trade unions is also in decline. In 2007 the Office for National Statistics reported a 3 per cent drop in union membership over the previous decade, a figure which partly disguises a larger drop in union membership among men (from over 35 per cent to under 28 per cent) (ONS, 2007a). Between 1964 and 2001 the Conservative Party misplaced over 1.5 million members, and the Labour Party lost one-third of its membership (Power Enquiry, 2006). Since 1997 electoral turnout in general elections has fallen by 20 per cent; in the 2005 general election 17 million registered voters stayed away from the polls (Electoral Commission, 2005). Some of this decline reflects a turning away from traditional sites of authority, and has benefited both smaller parties and political campaigning groups. The votes cast for 'other' parties have doubled since the 1970s, from about 3 per cent to about 6.5 per cent in the last 15 years. But the rise of smaller parties is not sufficient to make up for overall decline in participation. These trends reflect not only a fall in political participation but also a weakening of the role of political parties and trade unions in social identity. The 2007 British Social Attitudes survey reports a decline in 'very strong' and 'fairly strong' identification with political parties from 46 per cent in 1987 to 35 per cent in 2005, and a rise in those citing no party identification from 7 per cent in 1987 to 13 per cent in 2005 (Heath et al., 2007).

Social trends of this kind reflect changing patterns of behaviour and identity across the Western world. In Northern Europe and the USA there has been a general decline in religiosity, political participation, trade union membership, rates of marriage, newspaper readership and television viewing. At the same time there has been a general rise in new forms of religious practice, in smaller political parties and single-issue pressure groups, and in the use of new media forms. Although it is dangerous to read too much into such trends, they are perhaps indicative of a general malaise in attitudes towards traditional sites of authority. The shared value systems of prior ages are subject to increasing scepticism. In their place has emerged a fractured social experience, where dissent against traditional forms of authority occasionally hardens into religious and political fundamentalism, and where ideological formulations are replaced by a pick-and-mix approach to political, religious and theoretical ideas. In the digital age, the very idea of truth as an objective and collective experience seems to be in doubt.

Fractured truths

The apparent fracturing of shared value systems in contemporary culture exemplified by the kind of social trends touched on above has become a key component in post-modernist critiques of culture, which often associate the changing social landscape with a kind of nihilism where all values become equally mistrusted. Jean-François Lyotard, for example, has argued that the dominant condition of post-modernity is one of a growing 'incredulity towards metanarratives' (Lyotard, 1986: xxiv).[1] Metanarratives are the grand conceptual frameworks of the modern age, including science, religion, philosophy and political ideologies. As divergent and competing truth claims proliferate, the role of grand theory in validating what comes to be regarded as truth and knowledge declines. In its place people adopt a pick-and-mix approach to constructing individual outlooks, leading to a general decline in shared values, traditions and beliefs. Lyotard argues that this fragmentation of shared value systems results from a growing commodification of knowledge. As the 'use value' of knowledge is replaced by its 'exchange value', centres of knowledge production come under pressure to pursue truths solely on the basis of their marketability. Under these conditions, 'knowledge ceases to be an end in itself' (ibid.: 5) as its market value becomes more important to the production and dissemination of knowledge than the idea of objective truth.

Of particular importance for digital culture is the correlation Lyotard identifies between the transformations of knowledge in the post-modern age and the rise of communications and computing technology through the later part of the twentieth century. He argued:

> It is reasonable to suppose that the proliferation of information-processing machines is having, and will continue to have, as much of an effect on the circulation of learning as did advancements in human circulation (transportation systems) and later, in the circulations of sounds and visual images (the media). (Ibid.: 4)

Information-processing machines encourage the 'exteriorization of knowledge with respect to the "knower"' (ibid.); knowledge becomes associated not with what is known, but with the vessels that allow its exchange. Forms of knowledge that cannot be made to fit into the patterns of machine processing are in danger of being abandoned (ibid.). Lyotard believed this amounted to 'an internal erosion of the legitimacy principles of knowledge' (ibid.: 39); a crisis of legitimacy results from the erosion of the epistemological foundations of belief. He argued that 'the nature of knowledge cannot survive unchanged within this context of general transformation' (ibid.: 4). Knowledge is transformed to fit the patterns of the machine, and the fractured social experience becomes a by-product of this structural change to the dissemination of information.

Superficially this analysis appears to reflect the social experience of the late twentieth and early twenty-first centuries. With their decline, the traditional sites of authority through which metanarratives are perpetuated and authenticated are also subject to increased scepticism. However, the exteriorisation of knowledge that Lyotard describes is perhaps better understood as a characteristic of the modern age of Enlightenment rationalism. It was noted in Chapter 4 that by stabilising both individual textual works and the textual medium, printing resulted in the externalising of knowledge in relation to the individual. Printed artefacts were invested with performativity and authority in their own right, and as a consequence the idea of truth and authority was disinvested from the lived culture and reinvested in the documentary trace, resulting in an increased marginalisation of the oral tradition. Participation in knowledge creation, transmission and use became increasingly a matter of participation in literate modes of discourse; knowledge became associated with the vessels that allowed its exchange. This separation of knowledge from knowing through the reproduction of ostensibly identical printed works influenced the Enlightenment idea of objective mind-independent knowledge authenticated against the material reality it sought both to contain and to describe. While printing was neither a direct cause nor a necessary condition of the Enlightenment, the stability of the printed work was projected on to the idea of objective knowledge, secured neither against the social process nor against the individual mind, but against the external reality. Empirical science was privileged above social experience in this rationalist mode precisely because it could be authenticated in this way. The lived oral traditions in which knowledge was always contextualised within the social process and authenticated against memorial truths were subsumed beneath the rising edifice of science and engineering.

The central role of externalised forms of knowledge in Enlightenment rationalism suggests that the departure of post-modern culture from that rationalist ideal contains a complex interplay of knowledge and knowing, rather than merely the emergence of particular commodified forms as Lyotard implies. It is difficult to blame computers for a change in the status of knowledge arising from its exteriorisation if that exteriorisation precedes the digital age itself. At stake in the discourse of post-modernity therefore are not merely the particular forms of knowledge that constitute the material products of culture, but the changing social processes through which they are validated and exchanged. With its exteriorisation in the objects of culture through the modern age, control over knowledge became largely synonymous with control over the apparatus of its mediation; what came to be printed largely constituted the body of knowledge. The proliferation of communications technologies in the twentieth century pluralised ways of validating knowledge and sites of its creation, dissemination and use. This pluralising effect undermined the hegemony of the written word, leading to what Ong (1982) described as a secondary orality. However, while challenging the *structures* of media, for most of the twentieth century electronic communication technologies did not fundamentally shift the *processes* of mediation. Media production and transmission remained largely centralised within certain key sites. The content largely preceded its transmission, and was finalised before being consumed. Control over both mediation and the apparatus of mediation became synonymous with control over allowable knowledge and allowable truths.

In this book it is argued that social trends which indicate the decline of trust in traditional sites of authority result not from incredulity towards metanarratives, but from the conflict between narratives of different kinds, and between narratives and our lived experience. While the idea of truth has not lost its purchase within individual outlooks, how we understand the relationship between truth, social relationships and the artefacts of culture is challenged by changes to the ways in which we create and exchange information. The proliferation of digital technologies has initiated a rapid shift in the relationship between the apparatus of mediation that dominated the dissemination of information in the modern age and control over objective knowledge. It is in that shift that the declining trust in traditional sites of authority is situated. That decline is perhaps better described as only an *apparent* decline resulting from two interrelated structural changes: the proliferation of information, and a general disintermediation of knowledge creation and transmission made possible by digital technologies.

Information saturation

The explosion of information in digital culture is widely recognised. As information became more central to the functioning of the post-industrial economy, commodified through media and information services, it began to saturate the whole social process. All our actions in the digital sphere create traces in digital records, and much of our activity in digital contexts amounts to the creation and transmission of ever more information. Von Baeyer (2003) notes that the volume of recorded information in society has tended to follow a pattern of exponential growth, doubling roughly every 18 months. This means that not only is the volume always rising, but the rate of growth is also accelerating.

Digital technologies have exacerbated the trend towards information saturation in a number of ways. In the first place, new media and communication channels have supplemented existing provision. In 1997 just 17 per cent of UK households owned a mobile phone, but a decade later that proportion has risen to almost 80 per cent (ONS, 2007b). Since 1992 the number of webpages has risen from one single webpage to well over the 8 billion now indexed by the major search engines. E-mail, VOIP, SMS, MMS and instant messaging services have all added to the proliferation of communications platforms. While it is often argued that the future lies in platform convergence, throughout its history media technology has seen only an ever-increasing divergence. Secondly, changes to the regulatory environment accompanying technological development mean that more information now passes through the same communications channels than at any other time in history. Television channels, radio stations and telephone lines have multiplied with the emergence of digital services.

A consequence of this structural transformation to the dissemination of information is that we are each inundated with millions of individual messages every day. But while there is more information in culture than ever before, it is unclear that there is proportionately more original content; the demand for media and information exceeds the supply. In 1921 the editor of the *Manchester Guardian*, C.P. Scott, observed that 'comment is free, but facts are sacred', but today commentary plays a greater role in media and communications content than ever before, providing a way of eking out the meagre supply of new information, of adding value and creating market differentials. Much of the output of 24-hour news channels, for example, consists of comment and analysis; while the capacity of news broadcasting has grown, the volume of 'news' has not. More current-affairs programming is as a result provisional in nature, lacking the authoritative finalised nature of the nightly broadcast, always subject to emendation by developing events and always deferring judgements about its own significance. Similarly, the comment and analysis pages of national newspapers have tended to expand over time, with ever-increasing numbers of pundits, columnists and experts complicit in the reprocessing of already published information.

Structural changes to the media and publishing industries have transformed the marketplace of media production, resulting in a proliferation of content at the expense of original production. Although more television is broadcast on more channels, much of the programming of the digital age consists of repeats of programmes previously transmitted elsewhere. Although more books are published, a significant proportion are reissues of old editions that under the changing conditions of the marketplace become again commercially viable. An increasingly high proportion of the billions of pages that make up the web are aggregation services of different kinds that regurgitate content housed elsewhere, from click-through scams to price comparison sites. A *bricolage* digital culture is by its very nature invested in the reuse of existing information; much of the content on blogs and discussion groups is recycled from other sources, and the same videos are submitted to YouTube time and again. The *ennui* of post-modern culture perhaps reflects the sense that we have literally seen it all before.

In the context of its general proliferation and regurgitation, the cultural value of information cannot remain unchanged. Baudrillard (1994: 79) argued that 'we live in a world where there is more and more information, but less and less meaning'.[2] He suggested that 'the loss of meaning is directly linked to the dissolving, dissuasive action of information, the media, and the mass media' (ibid.). The proliferation of media forms and channels leads directly to a dislocation of meaning and the artefacts of culture; the meaningful cultural products of the past become replaced by simulacra empty of signifying value. As more information is produced, the value of any given piece of information declines. Searching for meaning and value in the intricate tangled web of digital culture has become one of the defining characteristics of the digital age.

Feather (2004: 113) argues that information has no scarcity value; a given piece of information does not lose its value by being more widely reproduced. This apparent lack of a scarcity value underpins in his view the tendency towards information saturation in digital culture; the robustness of information's value compels its endless reproduction. However, the scarcity value of information is in many contexts self-evident: stock market information is of greater value to a trader when more scarce because of the advantage it affords over other traders in a game of imperfect information; the cultural value of a first-edition book is greater precisely because first editions are often uncommon. Scarcity is effectively maintained through statutory frameworks such as intellectual property law which underpin the economic value of information by restricting copying and use.

This maintenance of scarcity is critical to the information economy because the value of information is always related to what is already known, and as a consequence restrictions in copying and use change that value. When in short supply, each nugget of information will have a proportionately greater impact on our understanding and knowledge, and thus its value will tend to be considered higher. But as we consume more information, each additional contribution makes a progressively smaller change to our understanding. The proliferation of information is therefore in Baudrillard's (1994) terms directly destructive of meaning, not because there is essentially less meaning invested in culture, but because each artefact contributes less to our total understanding and outlook. When the daily newspaper monopolised the circulation of news, each edition became critical to the outlook of individuals, influencing how they understood the world. When there were only two television channels, the public broadcaster could aspire to a Reithian ideal of public service. But as information channels proliferate, the contribution of any particular broadcaster or publisher to the wider culture declines. We are inundated with information, but in the process perhaps fail to derive additional value from it.

Disintermediation and remediation

The proliferation of information is just one aspect of the resituating of meaning and value for which digital technologies have been partially responsible. One of the most striking characteristics of digital culture is the general disintermediation of knowledge transmission and use. While in the age of publishing and mass media control over the apparatus of mediation became largely synonymous with control over discourse, digital technologies increasingly place power over the creation, dissemination and use of content in the hands of consumers. With disintermediation, the status of information and the relationship between the apparatus of mediation and control over knowledge begin to shift.

The general disintermediation of content dissemination is apparent on a number of different levels. In the first place, technology has changed the way in which we consume information and media content. DVD and hard-drive recorders have removed the temporal constraints on television viewing; video streaming and video on demand have placed the power of the scheduler into the hands of the viewer. With the declining cost of storage, more of the media products of culture are now available at our fingertips. We are in the digital age less subject to the drip-feed of information and media content, exercising more power over what we consume and when. Secondly, as the site of content creation has shifted closer to the site of its consumption, digital technologies have allowed users to compete with publishers and broadcasters in producing cultural capital. Websites and print-on-demand services excise the role of the publisher in the creation and dissemination of written works. The hegemony of news agencies has been broken with the emergence of blogging and citizen journalism, which both give expression to previously marginalised viewpoints. Social media services allow users to contribute their own media content; the word play of YouTube's legend, 'broadcast yourself', suggests how individuals become both the subject of their own media content and the controller of their own media production. With these technologies, a more participatory culture has emerged in which individuals contribute to the creation of information, knowledge and cultural artefacts through different modes of collaboration in the digital sphere. The dividing lines between the audience and broadcaster, reader and publisher, are beginning to blur.

Thirdly, with the ubiquitous network, the one-to-many model of content distribution exemplified by publishing and electronic media is being replaced by a many-to-many model exemplified by social software, from blogs to video-sharing services. Media content no longer radiates out from the epicentre of its production, but filters through society and culture by transmission between individuals within a social network. We all play a more active role in not only what kind of information and knowledge gets passed on, but also the make-up of that information and knowledge. Individuals intervene in content, reshaping, recontextualising and reconstructing its meaning. The cultural artefacts that emerge through this process tend not to participate in a single exemplar against which their authenticity and authority are secured, but mutate and change during the process of dissemination. Mediation in the digital age represents not the grand tributaries of the past in which the flow of knowledge runs through deep channels scored into culture, but a delta of numerous criss-crossing, interdependent shallow streams.

Through a process of remediation some of the qualities of this new participatory culture have been integrated into the traditional structures of media and publishing (Bolter and Grusin, 2000). Traditional media producers increasingly solicit the involvement of their consumers. Images captured on camera-phones record world events as they happen to those who experience them; the authenticity of much news in the twenty-first century derives from the quality of these amateur video clips. In addition, audience participation is encouraged across television and radio programming; text messages and e-mails are read out on air and interactive digital television services are reintegrated into television programming by being displayed in the same screen space. The viewer phone-in has become a mechanism not only of revenue generation, but also for involving the viewer in the programming. Television has as a result become more personal, not because it is tailored to our tastes and interests, but because by remediating new media interactive technologies it aspires to give the impression of a personal dialogue with the viewer. In a similar way the newspaper letters page has given way to the web-based discussion forum and the newspaper blog, where users not only read the news but also write it.

As participation becomes a normative mode of media consumption, the expectations of individuals about both their involvement in public discourse and their relationship to traditional sites of authority change. The proliferation of information through new media technologies has meant that individuals are able to engage in public discourse on something like an equal footing. While newspapers no longer report parliamentary speeches and debates in full, a criticism made by Tony Blair (2007) in his 'feral beasts' speech, the proceedings of Parliament are available unexpurgated on the web. The democratic success of the Hutton Inquiry (2004) derived not from its findings, which were subject to the kind of scepticism we should expect, but from the public availability of the evidence considered, made possible by web publishing. The availability of that evidence itself made the scepticism towards the findings of the inquiry more possible, and perhaps more likely. The public meeting has declined, but politicians reach out to voters through blogs and websites, bypassing traditional media outlets. With a greater part of the public record immediately accessible, the statements of those making claims to authority are more easily tested, and their inconsistencies readily exposed.

There is perhaps not too little truth in the digital age, but too much. As recorded information has proliferated, saturating the entire social process, competing truth claims jostle for attention and the idea of objective truth becomes more difficult to maintain. More information leads to a greater voicing of different and oppositional perspectives, outlooks and viewpoints as it becomes possible to express finer distinctions of belief and value. But in an age of disintermediation, claims to truth also become subject to greater scrutiny; every statement is met by a rebuttal, and every utterance undermined by a counterclaim. Scepticism perhaps becomes a dominant mode of participation and engagement, because in a cycle of self-reinforcement the more open voicing of dissent creates more grounds for uncertainty. When all claims to truth are constantly questioned, challenged and undermined, the very idea of objective knowledge itself becomes less secure.

Participatory culture and knowledge

In recent years much of the anxiety about the decline in objective truth has been concentrated in a wide-ranging and sometimes bad-tempered debate about the impact of Web 2.0 technologies on knowledge and culture. The idea of Web 2.0 derives from a paper by Tim O'Reilly (2005) that sought to summarise changes to web services in the early twenty-first century. O'Reilly's description of those changes is rather nebulous, focusing on themes rather than specific technologies; services such as wikis, blogs, RSS and Ajax are individually less significant than the underlying cultural mode they represent. The ethos of Web 2.0 centres on ideas such as 'hackability', 'the perpetual beta' and 'the long tail'. It is characterised by *play*, and by *trusting your users*. Web 2.0 becomes a matter of ceding control over applications, information and data to end-users, enabling them to reuse, create and disseminate knowledge and information in a more flexible and personal way. The shift in values this represents is associated with an *attitude* or *outlook*, reflecting the changing way in which information and knowledge are created, disseminated and consumed in the developed world. The idea of Web 2.0 therefore transcends the particular technologies on which it depends, reflecting a general shift in the dominant cultural mode that exemplifies for many the decline in the status of objective truth.

O'Reilly's account captures the essence of this new cultural mode, but is frustratingly short on detail. It is evocative without quite committing, making it difficult to bring the idea into sharp focus. The lack of detail is an essential part of Web 2.0's seductiveness, but has also compelled much criticism of the idea. Russell Shaw (2005) states 'the problem I have with this "Web 2.0" slogan is that it is a contrivance, meant to imply a unified movement or wave toward a better Web'. He argues that Web 2.0 represents little more than a means of marketing certain services. In a similar vein, John Dvorak (2006) said that 'Web 2.0 is the latest moniker in an endless effort to reignite the dot-com mania of the late 1990s'. Tom Wolfe has describe the blogosphere as 'a universe of rumours' (quoted in Rosenberg, 2007), and Nate Anderson (2006) recently posed the questions: 'In what sense do all the sites do something qualitatively different than the sites which came before? In what sense do these sites do anything similar enough that they can all be lumped into a single category?'

Perhaps the most vocal critic of Web 2.0 has been Andrew Keen, whose recent book *The Cult of the Amateur* (2007) scathingly critiques its consequences for knowledge and culture in the digital age. Keen contrasts the value of information and knowledge from traditional sites of authority, such as encyclopaedias, newspapers and publishers, with that which emerges through blogs, mash-ups and wikis. He argues that Web 2.0 technologies replace the expert with an army of amateurs, and substitute mediocrity and uncritical consensus for insight and imagination. The *bricolage* nature of contemporary digital culture undermines both creativity and talent; 'the ubiquitous remix is [...] destroying the sanctity of authorship' (Keen, 2007: 25). The participatory mode of digital culture blurs distinctions between truth and opinion, creating an 'undermining of truth' that threatens the quality of public discourse, encourages plagiarism and intellectual property theft and stifles creativity (ibid.: 17). This results in an 'infinitely fragmented culture in which we are hopelessly lost as to how to focus our attention and our limited time' (ibid.: 60). It also results in an undermining of notions of truth:

> Blogs have become so dizzying that they've undermined our sense of what is true and what is false, what is real and what is imaginary.

> These days, kids can't tell the difference between credible news by objective professional journalists and what they read on joeshmoe.blogspot.com. For these Generation Y utopians, every posting is just another person's version of the truth; every fiction is just another person's version of the facts. (Ibid.: 3)

Under these conditions, truth becomes just a version of fiction: the particular narratives to which people adhere in furtherance of their own interests or in pursuit of the validation of their own outlook. With the decline in the status of truth comes also the threat of the manipulation of the new mode of knowledge creation, dissemination and authentication by individuals and groups pressing particular political ends. Extremists, fundamentalists and criminals use the blurring of truth to perpetuate misinformation and lies. Like a kind of Lyotard-light for the digital age, Keen sees in the participatory mode only a cultural nihilism.

This attack on participatory culture relies on a number of sleights of hand that are worth detailing. Keen overestimates the objectivity of traditional media, journalism and publishing in order to contrast it with the subjectivity of participatory culture. Conversely, he underestimates the controls and guidelines provided by many Web 2.0 services, arguing, for example, that Wikipedia lacks any editorial guidelines or interventions (ibid.: 4). Secondly, he implies that the consumers of information are irrevocably subjugated by the messages to which they are subjected, barely able to distinguish truth from fiction and facts from lies, and almost wholly dependent on the integrity and objectivity of media producers for the veracity of the opinions and beliefs they form. Thirdly, he situates the creation of authority entirely within the structures of mediation, such as broadcasters and publishers, rather than in the creative acts that lead to information and knowledge, and the value they are given within culture. The decline of existing structures for the dissemination of information is therefore conflated with a decline in the quality of information itself. Fourthly, he constructs a false opposition between the expert and the amateur in order to dismiss the skill and expertise of amateurs. Many experts also contribute to collaborative modes of knowledge creation; and many amateurs have enviable knowledge and expertise. Quite when in Keen's opinion an amateur becomes an expert or how individuals earn the right of participation remain unclear, but it is implied that only a conferred authority, borrowed from the mediating structures of information dissemination and the traditional sites of authority, plays a part in determining the value of information and knowledge.

But notwithstanding this, what is really at stake in this anxiety about the consequences of a new participatory cultural mode is a distinction between two views of truth and knowledge. Traditionally, information has been understood as something that exists independently of cognition and social processes, a resource that can be drawn on to form opinions and beliefs. Information in this sense becomes in Buckland's (1991, 1997, 1998) terms a *thing*, not necessarily unanimous with the vehicles that contain it, such as books or websites, but objectively mind-independent. The *thing* of information can be sorted, classified, collected, stored and recorded because it is stable and enduring, not open to negotiation. The *thing* of information is authenticated against the external truths that it both contains and reflects. Similarly, knowledge has traditionally been viewed as something existing semi-independently of cognition and social processes, as if you could open up someone's head and pour the knowledge out. These ways of framing information and knowledge involve their objectification in two senses: they are both turned into objects and measured by their objectivity. That objectification exteriorises truth and knowledge in relation to the subject, and contributes to the investment of authority in institutions, mediating structures and individuals. Given truths that emerge from objective information and knowledge precede our personal knowledge of them and their dissemination; they can be handed down, transmitted and distributed. And given truths of this nature resist negotiation. Under these conditions, control over the apparatus of knowledge production and dissemination became synonymous with control over knowledge itself, and traditional sites of authority were granted a powerful hold over what came to be constituted as truth.

The rise of participatory culture undermines this sedimentation of objective knowledge in the vessels of its transmission and dissemination precisely because it undermines the stability of the cultural artefact itself. It is in this decline of certain mediating structures that the anxiety of a fragmentation of truths is invested; the loss of the stable vessels of objective knowledge threatens to undermine the Enlightenment project. But the investment of objective knowledge in the stable vessels that allow its transmission and dissemination has always been a kind of fiction, conflating knowledge with the structures of mediation. The authority of cultural artefacts has always involved a complex social process of negotiation between competing truth claims. The book does not become a site of authoritative knowledge by virtue of the conferred authority invested in it as a book, or by virtue of the conferred authority invested in its publisher or author. The value of the book is only ever that with which it is conferred in the complex process of its reception and assimilation into culture. Books that are widely read and widely valued, that seem to utter truths with which we can concur and which find their value within the whole cultural process, are granted an authoritative status; but that status is always conditional, liable to be withdrawn without notice as new ideas change the cultural context in which their meaning is discovered and understood. Books that fail to persuade within a particular cultural context are forgotten or overlooked. It is the claims to truth that are themselves negotiated in the reception of knowledge artefacts, not the prior status of the medium, author or publisher. Any trust that becomes invested in authors and publishers is only itself a conferred authority rooted in the perceived value of the works for which they are responsible.

Similarly, the television or radio programme is not a site of authority by virtue of the integrity of the television producer, but by being accepted and valued by its audience. The audiences of media, information and knowledge have always had a participatory role in creating and validating truths. As a kind of cultural shorthand, authors, publishers and broadcasters are conferred with a respect that properly belongs to the products for which they are responsible, and this often leads us to confuse the thing itself with its cultural value, resulting in mistaken assessments of the value, worth, objectivity or truth of particular cultural products. But it does not replace the authority invested in the work itself. The trust invested in the mediating structures is easily lost if the content itself comes under question, as exemplified by the recent scandals involving television phone-in competitions and the veracity of documentaries.[3]

The ideas of 'truth' and 'objective knowledge' were never really measured against external reality, as assumed within the Enlightenment mode, but against the social process in which truths are contested and opinions forged. This should not be taken to imply that claims to truth or authority are adjudicated along the lines of a popularity contest, the most widely disseminated ideas becoming those that make up received truths. Although the degree to which certain ideas are disseminated does influence the degree to which they are taken as truths, the process of validating knowledge involves a complex interaction of the documentary culture through which truth claims are transmitted and the lived culture in which they are accepted or rejected. Ideas emerge perhaps in the minds of individuals, but truths emerge through a wider social consensus. And the meaning of those truths mutates with the changing socio-cultural context and the shifting knowledge base.

While the structural changes to the creation, dissemination and use of information may have resulted in a pluralising of ideas and outlooks expressed within the documentary culture, that does not necessarily mean that the values and beliefs maintained by individuals within the shared social experience are themselves more fragmented. The digital age has not changed the nature of knowledge; it has merely changed the way in which we organise its creation and dissemination. Far from validating truths, the mediation of knowledge through traditional sites of authority celebrated by Keen (2007) merely acted to give the *impression* of shared values by imposing certain dominant outlooks on the visible recorded culture of the entire social system. The decline in objective truth is merely a fragmentation of this record of values and outlooks. Underneath the placid surface of the documentary culture of the modern age, the same churning of ideas and outlooks that characterises the post-modern condition was always under way. Participatory culture does not therefore by itself undermine objective truth; it merely exposes versions of truth as the socially situated claims that they always were.

The technologies of Web 2.0 reflect this recognition of the socially constructed nature of knowledge. They tacitly acknowledge that information and knowledge cannot be abstracted from the social processes with which they are irredeemably bound, but are in fact merely the essence, trace or record or those social processes. Through blogs, wikis and social networking, knowledge and information are constantly recreated and reconstructed. The knowledge base is constantly shifting, not only because we are continually adding to it, but also because existing knowledge is constantly reinvented in the light of social experience. The technologies of Web 2.0 seek to capitalise on that social dynamic to improve the quality of information services provision of various kinds. The information contained by the wiki is not independent of the use to which it is put or the sense that people make of it, but is constructed in the interactions of users. It becomes a constantly mutating text that reflects the changing understandings of its users. The folksonomy exploits the interaction of users with the information system itself to build constantly changing classification structures that resituate knowledge and information in line with the changing social environment. Meaning emerges through the social dynamic in which claims to truth are resituated and contextualised. The *impression* is that knowledge becomes less secure, outlooks more personally constructed and truths more relative, but in reality they always were.

Digital technologies have undermined the mediating apparatus through which control over knowledge was asserted in the modern age.

Through a general disintermediation in the creation and transmission of knowledge, control over discourse has been disinvested from the apparatus of knowledge creation and transmission and reinvested in the social process. Anxieties that centre on the decline of knowledge or loss of truth reflect a conflict between the values that emerged during the modern age, and which reflect a particular mode of knowledge creation and dissemination, and our lived experience in the digital age of a freer flow of information through culture. Disintermediation therefore changes not how we think about the idea of truth, but how we think about the relationship between truth and the artefacts of culture. It is simply certain mediating structures that are declining in the digital age, and not notions of truth or objective knowledge. These declining structures are those largely responsible for objectifying knowledge within a documentary trace. The book aspires to authority because it defers the point at which dissent is possible until after it has been fixed and finalised. The television programme aspires to authority because it defers the point at which dissent is possible until after it has been broadcast. But within the lived culture in which truths are negotiated and validated, dissent nevertheless always took place, and it is through dissent, disagreement and discussion that accepted truths emerge.

The digital age therefore really only represents a different way of organising the knowledge production, dissemination and authentication processes. While knowledge is no less secure, the processes through which knowledge comes to be authenticated are more open and exposed. The real difference in this new cultural mode is therefore not an ethos, an attitude or a technology, but an epistemological turn towards pragmatic constructivism in the consumption of cultural artefacts. The participatory mode of the digital age unites the documentary and lived cultures separated in the modern age.

Coming to knowledge in the digital age

While the pragmatic constructivist mode of knowledge authentication and transmission may not necessarily imply the danger of decline, it does perhaps necessitate that we reinvest in the critical process within which truth and knowledge have always been forged. In the age prior to print, literacy essentially meant participation in literate culture; the manner in which textual objects were contained by and apprehended within oral culture meant that the fine dividing line between orality and literacy was more difficult to draw. With the explosion of publishing, the oral contexts within which writing was contained declined and the oral and literate cultures became divorced, such that the ability to read became also a mechanism of social exclusion. Knowledge became the province of literate culture, and reading allowed access to that culture. Knowledge therefore became unanimous with the physical objects in which it was encoded, and access to knowledge entailed the ability to decode the meaning contained within those objects. In the age of mass publishing, the authority of written artefacts came under assault from the proliferation of texts. But literate culture responded by valorising particular cultural forms. The electronic age saw the rise of what Ong (1982) called a secondary orality contained in the technologies of television, radio, telephone and cinema. But this secondary orality did not replace literate culture in the way in which literate culture replaced, suppressed and marginalised oral culture. Authority and authenticity were still invested in material things. Literacy was still the ability to access and participate in the uses of writing.

But something is changing about the nature of authority in the digital age. How we interact with sites of authority and truth and how we understand information and knowledge are becoming less secure, less determinate and more fluid. This change emphasises the importance of both understanding the process of knowledge creation, transmission and use and critically evaluating the competing truth claims to which we are subjected. As we become deluged by information and claims to truth, the mode of authentication becomes reinvested in a critical participation in discourse. The value of first-order knowledge about *things*, including facts, data, theorems and information, declines in importance for the individual. In its place, the value of second-order knowledge about values, assumptions and aspirations increases. In the digital age, where information and data are cheap, proliferating through digital environments and always at the end of a search engine query, the value of knowledge derives from understanding the process through which truths become authenticated, and the underlying assumptions, values, biases, presuppositions and belief systems which inform that process.

This is captured in the idea of second-order literacy.[4] Second-order literacy is not a matter of reading, but of creating meaning out of texts or cultural objects within the whole social context. It is about situating truth claims within their social and cultural context and of reading the context as well as the content, not as a way of objectifying knowledge, but as a way of understanding truth claims. Second-order literacy is a matter of understanding that truths are never given, and that authority is never wholly conferred from the sites of knowledge production and creation. And second-order literacy is also a matter of participating in knowledge creation and dissemination, of participating in the process by which shared truths emerge. Within that second-order critical engagement, object truth and knowledge not only continue to have purchase, but become more central to our engagement with discourse.

Notes

1. See also Tredinnick (2006), Chapter 8.
2. See also Tredinnick (2006), Chapter 8.
3. 2007 was a year when stories about the faking of television documentaries and abuse of telephone competitions filled the UK news agenda. For a few examples see Robinson (2007); Holmwood (2007); Gibson (2007a, 2007b).
4. The more common term 'information literacy' is avoided to distance the idea from the a first-order knowledge about resources, tools and techniques, although it is recognised that information literacy is often associated with a *process* or *mode* of learning and engagement somewhat closer to what is described here (cf. Andretta, 2004).

7

Power

This chapter explores questions of power and its perpetuation in the digital age. The disintermediation of media appears on the face of it to have had a democratising effect, removing barriers to participation in discourse traditionally situated in the apparatus of knowledge and information creation and transmission. Where printing, mass media and mass-communication technologies generally acted to centralise the apparatus of knowledge production and transmission, digital technologies through their decentralising action perhaps effect the disinvestment of power from traditional sites of authority. However, it will be argued in this chapter that although some barriers to participation in digital culture have declined in importance, others continue to influence how power is wielded in the digital age. The visible structures of power perpetuated by the apparatus of media and communications have been replaced by the spider-web of the distributed digital network.

Power and discourse

One of the twentieth century's most influential theorists on questions of power and its perpetuation was the French post-structuralist theorist Michel Foucault.[1] He argued that power within society is always manifested in and perpetuated through forms of discourse. For Foucault, discourse does not just represent ways of speaking or writing, but the 'whole "mental set" and ideology which encloses the thinking of all members of society' (Barry, 2002: 176). Discourse provides a framework overlaying social structures that mediates both what comes to be regarded as knowledge and how it is disseminated and controlled. It therefore delimits not only what it is acceptable to say, but also what it is possible to say about given subjects at given points in time. Foucault argued that discourse is regulated by *epistemes*, the a priori historically situated theoretical frameworks that ground knowledge and truth. He wrote:

> I would define the episteme retrospectively as the strategic apparatus which permits of separating out from among all the statements which are possible those that will be acceptable within, I won't say a scientific theory, but a field of scientificity, and which it is possible to say are true or false. The episteme is the 'apparatus' which makes possible the separation, not of the true from the false, but of what may from what may not be characterised as scientific. (Foucault, 1980: 197)

Epistemes underpin power by regulating what comes to be constituted as knowledge. Different epistemes act to legitimise certain forms of knowledge at the expense of other outlooks, experiences and ideas. They therefore underwrite the perpetuation of power.

Foucault ([1991a] 1992: 60) believed that understanding the role of the episteme consisted in 'seeing historically how effects of truth are produced within discourses which are neither true nor false'. Different ways of categorising both phenomena and the relationships between phenomena represent different ways of framing allowable knowledge. In *The Order of Things* he outlined the influence of conceptual schemata on the structure of knowledge and knowing. Pre-modern and modern epistemes differ in privileging analogical and causal relationships respectively. While the analogical episteme of the pre-modern period strikes us as both strange and exotic, that strangeness also reveals the constraints on our own way of framing the relationship between things. In Foucault's (1970: xvi) view, different legitimate ways of seeing the world exist, perpetuated through the structural order imposed on phenomena through discourse; these differences represent classifications derived not from the properties of things but from ways of interpreting the relationships between them. Rather than lacking reason, as often implied, pre-modern thought reflects only a different kind of reasoning.

Foucault's notion of discourse is tied up with language use, and much of his analysis centres on how language is deployed to control and perpetuate existing power relations. In *The Order of Things* he wrote:

> Language forms the locos of tradition, of the unspoken habits of thought, of what lies hidden in a people's mind; it accumulates an ineluctable memory which does not even know itself as memory.

> Expressing their thoughts in words of which they are not the masters, enclosing them in verbal forms whose historical dimensions they are unaware of, men believe that their speech is their servant and do not realize that they are submitting themselves to its demands. The grammatical arrangements of a language are the *a priori* of what can be expressed in it. (Ibid.: 324)

White (1979: 85) argued that Foucault denied the concreteness of the symbolic referent and rejected the notion that there is a 'reality' which precedes language. Harland (1987: 101) similarly observed that 'he rejects the notion of truth as a correspondence of ideas to things'. Foucault rejected the idea that truth precedes its expression; the effects of truth are created within discourse. Language is the precondition of knowledge creation and transmission, and locks into its structures certain dominant conceptual forms that constrain what comes to be expressible and what comes to be regarded as objective truth. This has led to accusations of linguistic determinism (Chandler, 2002). But discourse is not just a matter of language; it saturates the whole social situation and is perpetuated through institutions, practices and social relations. Foucault's (1972) *archaeological* method, to be distinguished from a traditional historical method that implied the narration of experiences from a position of power and privilege, was developed in a series of alternative histories: *The Order of Things* (1970), *Madness and Civilisation* (1967), *Discipline and Punish: The Birth of the Prison* (1977) and *The History of Sexuality* (1979, 1984a, 1984b). These sought to undercut received historical understanding by highlighting the histories of the disempowered.

Foucault's analysis of power is important to how we understand the structural changes to knowledge creation and dissemination in the digital age. The disintermediation of discourse explored in the previous chapter has led some theorists to argue that digital technologies have had a democratising effect, disinvesting power from the traditional structures through which it is mediated and controlled, and reinvesting it in the social process. An impression of something like this view may have been given in the previous chapter. Because digital technologies allow in principle a more equal participation in the structures of discourse, they perhaps also overcome the marginalisation of certain world-views within society and culture: individuals and groups excluded from the apparatus of knowledge creation and transmission in the age of print and electronic media are able to access this apparatus in the digital age. Through the use of blogs, wikis, websites and social networking services, we all perhaps become complicit in the construction of allowable knowledge. However, Foucault's analysis of discourse suggests that power is insidious, finding a way to assert and perpetuate itself through different kinds of social structure. Because discourse saturates the whole social process, the structural changes to knowledge creation and dissemination are unlikely to reflect a simple dissipation of power across the social system.

Preconditions of participation

Power over participation in the formation of discourse is not merely a matter of particular claims to power articulated through social capital, privilege and prestige, but also a matter of the underlying social structures that mediate social interaction. Old limitations on access to discourse were based in part on access to the structures through which it was perpetuated and maintained: not only the media and publishing industries, whose influence was highlighted in the preceding chapter, but also social institutions such as the university, political party, trade union or religious body. These structures create what Althusser ([1971] 2006) termed the 'Ideological State Apparatus', and represent 'not only the *stake*, but also the *site* of class struggle'. In other words, competing ideologies seek dominance not only within these spheres, but also through manipulating them.

It has been noted that by centralising the process of knowledge creation and dissemination, printing and later the electronic media acted to make control over knowledge largely synonymous with control over the apparatus of its transmission and dissemination. The point at which dissent became possible was shifted to the moment of knowledge consumption. By bringing together the moment of creation and the moment of consumption, digital technologies on the face of it act to decentralise control over knowledge and discourse, reinvesting power over discourse in the whole social process. However, while this may represent a structural change in certain channels through which power is mediated, it does not necessarily represent a fundamental shift in the basis of power. Two questions emerge in relation to the perpetuation of power in the digital age: what kind of preconditions are there to participation in digital culture, and what values come to underpin the valorisation of certain kinds of knowledge over others?

While some structural barriers to participation decline in the digital age, others persist. Digital computers, mobile phones and network connection are the new apparatus of knowledge creation and dissemination. Participation in digital culture is dependent upon access to and use of these technologies, but neither access nor use is equally distributed. This is often known as the digital divide, although it is perhaps better described as the digital *divides*, as it consists of a number of interrelated elements.[2] First come the infrastructural inequalities that persist in the distribution of access points and network density in different parts of the world. The internet may be a global information system, but it is not evenly distributed. Network density is highest within the USA, Western Europe and parts of East Asia; it is at its lowest in continental Africa. Mobile telephone network density is highest in the developed world and lowest in the developing world. Major communication lines and satellite links tend to connect parts of the developed world with one another. The uneven distribution of the digital infrastructure creates structural inequalities in access to the digital superhighway; more digital information is disseminated more rapidly across the developed world than across the developing world. Equally important are global differences in levels of internet use and of available technology. The number of computers per head of population and the integration of technology into people's day-to-day lives correlate with the relative wealth of nations. The map of the internet more or less reflects the spread of economic and political power across the globe.

The uneven distribution of both resources and infrastructure highlights how on a global basis some cultures, traditions and values have a greater voice in digital culture than others. Through its dominance over the new apparatus of participation, the developed world asserts its values and traditions in the digital sphere. The greater presence of certain values and traditions in digital culture contributes to their self-reinforcement; such values become the norm against which other contributions are measured. This is not necessarily an intentional outcome, but a reflection of uneven access to the new mechanisms of power in the digital age. While there may be no intention to marginalise certain forms of knowledge, through the aggregation of our individual behaviour, values and traditions, filtered through different degrees of access and participation, the structural imbalances in access result in equivalent imbalances in the voices that are heard and represented in the digital sphere.

One significant aspect in this sifting of power relations emerges through the linguistic distribution of digital content. Although precise figures are difficult to estimate, about 40 per cent of all web content is written in English and therefore only accessible to English speakers (Paolillo et al., 2005). Around 20 per cent is written in one of the other major European languages: French, German, Spanish, Italian and Portuguese (ibid.). All other world languages make up just over one-third of all web content (ibid.). The lack of linguistic variety both reflects and reinforces the uneven nature of participation in digital culture. It derives from the aggregation of individual participation, and it results in structural advantages for native speakers of those languages that are most dominant. While some challenge to the hegemony of the developed world does emerge through different kinds of digital discourse, these challenges are always contained by the structural dominance of particular outlooks, traditions and beliefs. Content in minority languages (minority by representation, not importance) is more likely to be overlooked.

The uneven global distribution of digital technologies threatens to lock in the economic advantage of the developed world. Castells (2001) and Negroponte (2005) have both argued that the only way to tackle this global inequality is to concentrate resources on developing the technological infrastructure and knowledge base of the developing world. They argue that by encouraging technological development, the economies of the developing world can leapfrog their way into the twenty-first century, acquiring the skills base and expertise to compete in a global digital economy. However, this view has been challenged by aid organisations and charities, which stress the need for investment to be concentrated on basic services such as healthcare, sanitation, schooling and water supply. Cullen (2001) notes: 'For the majority of the world's population, telephones are a technology beyond reach; food, sanitation and literacy are more urgent.' From this perspective, projects like Negroponte's $100 laptop (now $200) threaten to sap resources and commitment from addressing the real needs of the developing world.

The issues in this debate are highly charged, and it is not an argument to be joined lightly. However, ultimately perhaps the global digital divide exists because it suits the West, and unless or until it suits the developed world to have a more equal distribution of global wealth that divide will be perpetuated. As a consequence, control over discourse becomes largely a matter of what knowledge and truths suit the industrialised countries. This should not be taken to imply that the marginalisation of the developing world is imposed by central authorities, such as the World Bank, World Intellectual Property Organization, European Union or individual governments, each acting to perpetuate its own power, although this is also a factor. Rather it should be taken to imply that through the aggregation of individual decisions, behaviour and action within the digital sphere the structural imbalance is perpetuated. We are all complicit in the creation of a global digital divide, whether we mean to be or not.

The difference in barriers to participation is an issue that affects not only the digital divide *between* nations but also the digital divide *within* nations.[3] On the whole, cities are better connected than rural economies. In the UK high-capacity broadband services are concentrated on metropolitan and suburban environments. WiFi access points tend to cover urban centres. Mobile phone coverage is denser in UK cities and towns than in the countryside, and least dense in parts of Scotland and Wales. The People's Network providing free internet access at UK public libraries tends, like the library service itself, to be concentrated in urban areas. Some of this uneven distribution simply reflects the law of supply and demand, but it is also the case that the cost of service provision is usually greatest in those areas where population density is lowest, and this militates against uniformity of provision. The concentration of digital services in some geographical areas tends to lead to an associated demand for skills and more opportunities to develop those skills. The uneven distribution can thus have the effect of locking in technological advantage, leading to a concentration of industry and services in urban areas and a decline of the rural economy.

Barriers to participation in digital culture are not just infrastructural in nature, but also reflect socio-cultural differences.[4] In the UK, income, age, social class, gender, disability and level of education all correlate to levels of access to and use of digital technologies. The idea of the 'silver surfer' may have become a part of the discourse of digital culture, but the over-65s are still the lowest-represented demographic group considered in terms of access to digital culture. Although the gaps between the haves and the have-nots of the digital age are declining over time, with current trends it will take decades to address the social divides manifested within the digital domain, and the rate at which the gap is narrowing is itself slowing down. Demographic differences in levels of access and use of digital technologies also impact on the kinds of use made of technologies by individuals, and consequently their degree of participation in digital culture. Younger age groups, for example, are more likely to blog and use wikis and social networking services. Again there is an issue of familiarity and education. The fewer the barriers to participation and use, the greater the familiarity with and trust invested in digital services of different kinds. Access to the new apparatus of discourse is therefore also constrained by social inequalities that generally map on to existing lines of power and control.

This highlights the very real difficulty involved in addressing the demographic digital divide. Many programmes focus on removing structural barriers to access. The People's Network, for example, made free access to internet-ready digital computers available across the UK. Other programmes have focused on user education to overcome the socio-cultural barriers to participation. But these attempts can only ever be a partial solution, because the real barriers to participation in digital culture are more deeply ingrained within the social system and global economy. Different components of the digital divide reinforce one another and reflect more deeply entrenched social inequalities. The People's Network, for example, presupposes familiarity with libraries and library services. While it has helped to raise use of library services, particularly among certain demographic groups such as the young and migrant communities, it is nevertheless the case that public library use is itself tied to social demographics. Crossing the threshold of a library is for some of the most socially disadvantaged members of society itself a step too far because of the bureaucratic power and traditional social values that the library itself can inadvertently represent. The real divide is not technological in nature, but a matter of the distribution of opportunity and power within society.

Participation and power

The kinds of inequalities in participation within digital culture touched on above do not determine the lines of power over discourse in the digital age, but highlight how the interests of certain groups tend to be perpetuated through any available structures. Demographic differences contain and reflect more general patterns of social inequality that create barriers to participation of different kinds. Underpinning the digital divide are three universals of participation in culture: money, time and education. On the whole, the more wealthy, educated and time-rich we are, the greater our ability to participate in the formation of discourse and contribute to the cultural sphere of digital environments. These fundamental preconditions of participation are not particular to digital culture, and in this respect the digital divide is no different from other kinds of social inequalities and divisions. Power over digital discourse is not determined by *access* to the apparatus of knowledge creation and transmission; on the contrary, *access* is determined by power.

These underlying preconditions on participation in digital culture play an important role in how we understand the nature of digital discourse and the limitations of technology in addressing inequalities in power. For example, Castells (2001) argues that the wider use of communications technology brings with it a new meritocracy of employment. Drawing on Bell's (1974) model of the post-industrial society, he argues that as knowledge and information become more important to the network organisation, the value of individual employees is shifted from what they do to what they know. With this comes the idea of the portfolio career, where individuals develop work profiles built out of many different concurrent or sequential individual roles in different organisational settings. The move towards short-term and contract employment therefore also represents an opportunity for individuals to market themselves on the basis of their knowledge and experience. Flexibility, critical thinking and the ability to learn become more central to employment success. This emphasises the role of education in the new economy. Because these skills are not dependent on demographic social differences, success in the new flexible employment marketplace depends less on old social divisions of class, gender and ethnicity, and more on the expertise, abilities and value that the individual can bring to the organisation.[5]

However, Castells (2001) fails to recognise that the risks and benefits of the portfolio career are not evenly distributed. It is not the case that educational opportunity and flexibility of employment are unconstrained by traditional social inequalities; the same social divisions that influenced employment practices in the age of the job for life also influence employment practices in the age of the portfolio career. Critical to taking advantage of the opportunities afforded by flexible working practices and the portfolio career is the freedom to take risks with employment. Success in the digital age depends in part on how far one is willing to countenance failure. The opportunities offered by flexible working practices are therefore disproportionately weighted towards those who are able to take risks. But the degree of risk implied by flexible working practices is not itself absolute; different personal circumstances change how much risk is associated with flexible working. The portfolio career will generally favour individuals without dependants and with financial security, who have the luxury of picking and choosing between opportunities that present themselves. It will disadvantage those with dependants or those without financial security, for whom the risk of the short-term contract is outweighed by the benefits of the stable job. The socially advantaged are emancipated by flexible working patterns, but the socially disadvantaged are locked into patterns of insecure short-term employment. Similarly, access to education depends not only on immediate funding, but also on the balance between future rewards and present realities. The long-term benefit of education is neither here nor there if your immediate circumstances are such that there is simply no scope to make that investment of time, money and short-term security. Therefore educational level is often just as much a marker of class and social status as other social demographic indicators. The same social constraints reassert themselves in the supposed new meritocracy of work.

This highlights how power perpetuates itself through any available structures: whatever apparatus mediates the creation and dissemination of knowledge and information, and participation in digital culture, the same social groups tend to benefit. Underpinning access to the new digital apparatus of knowledge creation and transmission are the same social inequalities that determined access to the old apparatus of centralised broadcasting and publishing, academia, government and employment success. Digital technologies may have led to a disintermediation of knowledge creation and transmission, but they have not led to a fundamental shift of power within society. This is not to imply that the aspiration to reduce or remove social inequalities is naïve or doomed to failure, but rather that as the social context changes new forms of disadvantage and marginalisation will always assert themselves. Some individuals, social groups and nations will always transcend these structural lines of power; Postman (1992) has argued that in the digital age there will be both winners and losers, but nevertheless we do not all start from equal positions. Thus, although we can perhaps say that there has been a pluralising of access to discourse, we cannot say that there has been a democratising of discourse. More people may participate in the construction of truths and knowledge, but that greater plurality is not necessarily any more representative of the socio-cultural system as a whole. Digital culture has democratised participation for certain already privileged groups, but also perpetuates the existing social inequalities within the wider social system.

The structure of digital discourse

If the preconditions of participation in digital culture are not fundamentally different from those in the media age, do the values of digital discourse themselves lead to a democratising of culture? In the previous chapter it was argued that a pragmatic constructivism comes to underpin how information and knowledge are authenticated in the digital age. It could therefore be argued that this represents the *episteme* of the digital age: the underlying structure of digital discourse that influences both what ideas can be expressed and how they can be expressed. However, pragmatic constructivism implies merely a *mechanism* for the reinvestment of authenticity and authority; it does not describe the values that play a part in that process. Keen (2007: 92) commented: 'The irony of a "democratized" media is that some content producers have more power than others.' The value attributed to the contributions of different people within digital culture is not equal. Some voices are afforded more emphasis and consideration than others.

An important aspect of the distribution of power over digital discourse is the way in which judgements about the credibility of individual contributions to digital culture are formed. The credibility of cultural artefacts in the modern age was in part influenced by the indexical association between content and form, and incorporated a conferred credibility forged in the link maintained between the original creative act and the mechanical reproduction that acted as a kind of shorthand in the evaluation of individual artefacts or information. With both disintermediation and the separation of material and form, this extrinsic means of validating knowledge has become more problematic. This kind of source credibility continues to play an important role in individual experiences of the web; commercial interest, design and usability and the conferred credibility of organisations or individuals invested with *trustworthiness* all play a part in how users assess the credibility of web content (Metzger et al., 2003). However, source credibility is problematised by the *bricolage* nature of participatory culture and the dematerialising of cultural artefacts.

Flanagan and Metzger (2007) note that 'perceptions of credibility can be highly situational and may depend on the receiver's relationship to the medium, the source of the message, and the message itself'. Fogg (2003) developed a prominence-interpretation model of online credibility judgements that involves an interaction of the prominence of the message with the individual's judgement about that message based on assumptions in the users' minds, their skills and experience and their situational context. This model emphasises the negotiation between the message and the reader in assessments of the credibility of new media. Metzger et al. (2003) discussed four elements of message credibility: structure, content, language intensity and message delivery. These studies all highlight the multifaceted nature of credibility judgements in the digital age, but they also highlight how the way in which a message is received also depends on the nature of that message and perceptions about the trustworthiness and expertise of the source of that message. Flanagan and Metzger (2007) noted that the burden of assessing information has been placed 'squarely on the shoulders of the media consumer'.

Credibility judgements of digital content tend to be made on the basis of both the intrinsic qualities of the text or work and how that text or work fits into the individual's outlook. The credibility of a blog posting or a wiki page depends on the negotiation between its content and the wider knowledge and understanding of the person reading that content, including knowledge and understanding of both the page itself and the people or groups responsible for it. In digital participatory culture these judgements become complicit with digital identity; both who we claim to be in the digital domain and how we are perceived influence the way in which our contributions to discourse are framed and understood. Part of this relates to the continuity and consistency of our presence. Presence allows the delineation of particular spheres of expertise that come to underpin the value attributed to our contributions. But presence in digital spheres is disjunctive: our presence in one domain may have no impact on how we are perceived in other domains. The credibility that may come to be invested in our contributions to a particular wiki may have no influence on our contributions to other wikis, to the blogosphere or to discussion forums. Presence therefore often reduces to a series of messages in discrete domains that are hard to secure against modes of authentication of traditional media and knowledge artefacts. The credibility of digital content is thus invested in a radical trust forged through interactions in the digital sphere – radical because it is a trust based on the conventions of digital discourse as much as on actual social transactions. The structure of digital discourse influences the kind of value that is attributed to different contributions.

Different discourses generate different ways of speaking about the world that act to legitimise certain viewpoints, outlooks and experiences. Part of this is a matter of the technical jargon that accompanies different speaking or writing situations; fields of knowledge develop their own technical vocabulary that marks out different kinds of speakers and acts to legitimise certain kinds of contribution. But it is not just through the vocabulary of discourses that control is reinforced; it is also reinforced through the norms of participation, exchange and argument and the assumed prior knowledge of participants. Eagleton (1996: 175) commented about the discourse of literary criticism:

> Becoming certified by the state as proficient in literary studies is a matter of being able to talk and write in certain ways. It is this which is being taught, examined and certified, not what you personally think or believe, though what is thinkable will of course be constrained by the language itself. You can think or believe what you want, as long as you can speak this particular language.

Jenkins (1991) made a similar point about the discourse of history. Expertise has always been a matter of the mastery of the language games of different intellectual and cultural traditions.[6]

Technical vocabulary, norms of participation and the assumed prior knowledge of participants are all important to the nature of digital discourse, acting to legitimise some contributions and marginalise others. Chapter 4 noted how text in the digital sphere is becoming more mutable, with an increased use of acronyms and emoticons to mediate expression. These are just a part of the technical vocabulary of the digital sphere; mastering digital discourse is in part a matter of understanding the particular language within which particular ideas are expressed. It was also noted that the more informal use of text in digital information contexts creates a discourse that is situated somewhere between the oral and literary traditions. The use of performative gestures, particularly transactional utterances, becomes a part of the norms of participation. It is also the case that certain cultural reference points tend to dominate digital discourse. Behind the folksonomy or the wiki, for example, are ideas about the emergence of order out of chaos that derive from complexity theory. Cyberculture still glistens with allusions to Douglas Adams and Monty Python. Anyone unfamiliar with the game Mornington Crescent and its origin in the radio show *I'm Sorry I Haven't A Clue* is likely to find its online incarnation incomprehensible. Shibboleths in jokes, shared games and cultural touchstones all play an important role in participation in digital spheres, and increasingly discrete conventions of digital discourse are emerging in different realms.

Therefore, although credibility judgements in digital contexts are less dependent on the kind of conferred credibility derived from social status, employment and expertise, this does not mean that all contributions to digital culture are equal; it does not result in a discourse where 'every posting is just another person's version of the truth; every fiction is just another person's version of the facts' (Keen, 2007: 3). Just as in the age of print and electronic communication, some versions of truth come to dominate, and through their dominance perpetuate their own narrative view of truth and knowledge. The ability to participate in digital culture on something like an equal footing is dependent on not only access to digital technologies but also an understanding of the rules and conventions of participation. It is not just the *language* of digital discourse that comes to mediate power and participation, but the language games and their tacit, unarticulated and often incomprehensible rules. All views do not become equal; power is disinvested from the apparatus of knowledge creation and transmission, but it is reinvested in control over content. In many digital information contexts the message supersedes the medium.

Power anxieties

The effect of digital technologies on the way in which power and control are exercised and perpetuated can in some ways be thought to be rather pernicious, blurring the clearer lines of power that were present in previous ages. The centralised apparatus of knowledge creation and dissemination has been replaced by a spider-web of social relationships, status and degrees of participation. But this apparent perniciousness of digital inequalities perhaps merely reflects the readjustment of power and control in the digital age; as the influence of digital technologies becomes something to which we are more accustomed, the lines of power will perhaps seem no less obvious that those perpetuated in the media age. The role of the news agency in authenticating what comes to be counted as 'news', for example, may be declining in the digital age, although not perhaps to the degree that is often suggested, but just because we have as yet no very clear assessment of the way in which blogs contribute to authenticating what comes to be counted as 'news' does not mean that similar processes are not already in play. The readjustment of power is perhaps still sifting through the entire social system, restructuring individual relationships between people, social groups, organisations and nation-states. The final shape of power and its perpetuation in the digital age are yet to be revealed.

However, we can begin to say something about how the perpetuation of power is changing in the digital age. Disintermediation has resulted in the disinvestment of power from control over the apparatus of knowledge creation and transmission, and its reinvestment in control over content. As a consequence, information aggregation services of different kinds become increasingly important to the shape of power in the digital age. Search engines, social networking sites, social media sites and network service providers in principle wield almost immeasurable control over discourse and knowledge. With half of all search queries going through it (Burns, 2007), Google has in principle an almost unlimited capability to determine not only what information matters, but also what information most users ever get to see. But the power of the information vendor, unlike that of the software house or hardware manufacturer, exists largely in principle and not in practice. While software and hardware create their own economic lock-in effects, information services generally do not. Google's dominance of the search market depends on the trust invested in it by users. The decision of the individual to turn to a particular search engine today will not substantially commit them to turning again to that same search engine tomorrow. Convergence in the search, aggregation and social networking sectors means that most services essentially work in the same way. A new operating system has first to overcome the market saturation of Microsoft Windows before its value can be fully realised. A new search engine simply has to do web searching better.[7] Google is in fact atypical in retaining its dominant market position for a decade, but even Google originally overturned the goliaths of search from a garage workshop (Google, 2007). Innovation always has the potential to rewrite the existing rulebook of power and influence when the site of control is invested in content and not in infrastructure.

Williams (1980) argued that under hegemonic domination emergent and oppositional forms are reincorporated into the values of the dominant culture, and in the process they are disarmed of their oppositional sting. This process of emergence and incorporation in many ways exemplifies the development of digital culture. Services such as YouTube, Facebook, Digg and Bebo rise in the space of months from conception to market dominance. But as YouTube and Facebook emerged as dominant forces, each was acquired by already established market players. As new forms emerge and threaten to undermine traditional lines of power and control, those forms are quickly incorporated into existing structures. The emergence of the blog, for example, threatened perhaps to undermine the status of traditional journalism, but the blog was rapidly incorporated into the output of news outlets as newspapers and broadcasters started to publish blogs of their own. Similarly, file sharing and digital downloads challenge the control of publishers over content, but are rapidly incorporated into the publishing industry through authorised download sites and e-content provision.

This process of emergence and incorporation involves a kind of negotiation between the dominant and emergent cultural forms: the incorporation of emergent cultural forms changes the dominant culture. Through incorporation, conferred credibility reasserts itself in the pragmatic mode of knowledge construction and transmission. As newspapers and television broadcasters start their own blogs, the cultural status of both the newspaper and the blog shifts. The incorporation of new media forms ties credibility judgements back to the traditional structures of media and publishing. But again in this is a negotiation between traditional sites of authority and the values of the new media forms they incorporate; the values of traditional media are not imposed on new media forms, but are changed by the incorporation of those forms. This negotiation brings with it the inculcation of existing values into the new structures of discourse – values that themselves tend to perpetuate inequalities. The blog and the wiki emerged with egalitarian aspirations of a more even distribution of power over discourse, but as soon as they come actually to *matter* they will tend to be incorporated into existing social structures of power and control. The mode of authentication is changed, but existing sites of power and control learn how to win within that new cultural mode.

If digital culture does not reflect the seeds of a new democratic organisation of society and social participation, it does perhaps reflect a sifting and resorting of existing lines of power and influence significant in its own right. The rise of the digital network has tended to shift the boundaries of discourse, and has resulted in anxieties about the perpetuation of power in the digital age. With the proliferation of transborder flows of information, the cultural and legal integrity of the nation-state is beginning to crumble. Information is now distributed across the globe without boundaries, transcending the control of national legal and regulatory frameworks. Identity is less rooted in nationality (Castells, 2000), and social and political groups and associations are more able to coordinate their activities on a global scale. The worldwide anti-war protests in 2002 and 2003 and the annual May Day anti-globalisation protests testify to the globalisation of political movements and political identity. Information also flows more freely out of countries with repressive regimes; the global coverage of the democracy protests in Burma in 2007 reflects the reach of mobile phones and internet access. It is telling that one of the first actions of the military junta was to close down mobile phone networks and internet service providers (Thompson, 2007). The so-called Great Firewall of China echoes the threat posed by this free flow of information and ideas to existing lines of power and control. But the Great Firewall is only the most manifest form of power anxiety in the digital age; all governments face a challenge to their authority, a challenge which is a kind of scaling up of the micro-anxieties over knowledge, intellectual property and the fragmentation of culture and identity.

This globalisation of some aspects of discourse leads to its own conflicts and anxieties as different cultural norms, values and taboos come face to face in the digital domain. But the reach of the digital network also poses challenges and threats, from the rise of global terrorism to the growth of organised crime and international criminal gangs. The other side of the freedom and access to discourse made possible by digital culture is the very public opportunity to distribute materials that would seem to undermine the freedom the digital network secures, from videos of roadside bombings and beheadings in Iraq to pornography and extremist political messages. The global network is a new frontier, largely without effective regulation, where ethical and criminal responsibility is increasingly placed on the users of information freely published, rather than on its distributors or publishers. The global reach of the network means that within individual legal and regulatory territories, only access to and use of materials can be controlled. The interconnectedness of digital discourse fuels anxieties about threats that are essentially beyond national control.

This perhaps explains some of the emerging fears in the digital age. The threat of global terrorism, for example, can in part be understood as a reaction against the disintermediation of discourse. The response of the UK government to this perceived threat has been at least in part a matter of increased control over different aspects of society: migration, information transmission, individual movements and assembly, and identity. The dangers of the network society are perhaps exaggerated by traditional sites of power precisely as a means of retaining power that is threatening to drain away from the traditional apparatus of regulation and control. Ideas, ideologies and writings become feared as explicitly as the terrorist acts they underpin and propound; while the flow of ideas and written materials cannot be stemmed, their possession can be criminalised. The UK Terrorism Act 2006 (s. 2(3)), for example, criminalises possession and dissemination of 'any matter which is likely to be useful in the commission or preparation of [terrorist] acts', a definition so wide as potentially to cover any number of items previously freely distributed both digitally and in paper, from the notorious *Anarchists Cookbook* to maps, sightseeing guides and lists of tourists attractions. Castells (2001) argued that an inevitable rebalancing of freedom and surveillance is necessary in an interconnected digital age. This may perhaps be the case, but it is also becoming clearer that the limits of freedom and control in the digital age come under increasing scrutiny precisely because of the restructuring of power. The global political flux of the twenty-first century is itself a reflection of the resifting of power in the disintermediated digital age.

Notes

1. See also Tredinnick (2006), Chapter 7.
2. The international and national digital divides have been subject to extensive research. Although the precise levels of participation have tended to change over time, the underlying trends are relatively consistent. For some recent studies underpinning this discussion, see Castells (2000, 2001, 2004), Bromley (2007) and Dutton and Helsper (2007).
3. For some recent studies underpinning this discussion see Castells (2000, 2001, 2004), Bromley (2007), Dutton and Helsper (2007) and ONS (2007b).
4. Castells (2001) reports a similar pattern in the USA.
5. The idea of a new meritocracy of employment is not merely an abstract sociological theory, but has become a part of the political policy agenda, underpinning the discourse of the knowledge economy and the shift of the burden of funding higher education on to the individual.
6. See also Tredinnick (2006), Chapter 5.
7. If you are already the market leader it is far easier to invest in better search technologies, and familiarity with a service is a disincentive for users to move elsewhere, so some mechanisms for the self-reinforcement of market position do continue to play a role in the digital age.

8

Identity

Just about the most widely cited critique of the nature of identity in the digital age was published in the *New Yorker Magazine* in July 1993. A cartoon by Peter Steiner portrayed two dogs in front of a desktop computer. The caption read: 'On the internet, nobody knows you're a dog' (Steiner, 1993). The joke plays on two truisms of digital culture: that identity is both self-consciously constructed and more liquid in digital environments. The faces that we show to the world are not only varied and context-dependent, but generally a matter of how we present ourselves rather than how we are perceived by others. This chapter explores questions of identity in the digital age. It will examine not only what identity means, but also the systematic virtualisation of identity that has accompanied digital information contexts, and its consequences for social organisation and interaction.

The nature of identity

The nature of *identity* is both complex and contested. In psychology identity is often used to describe either a sense of self or the characteristic qualities that make individuals who they are. It is also used to describe the ties individuals forge with the social roles that they play: parent, child, spouse, employer, colleague and so on. Within social science, identity is generally associated with the ways in which people label themselves or come to be labelled as members of social groups on the basis of shared values, experiences or characteristics. This idea gives rise to identity politics, or political action intended to advance the position of certain social groups, usually those marginalised by society. Self-identity is therefore inseparable from the social contexts in which it is forged. Barker (2002: 109) has written:

> Identities are wholly social constructions and cannot 'exist' outside of cultural representations that constitute rather than express

identity. Subsequently it is from the plasticity of identity that its political significance flows.

Identity is something both constructed by individuals in their interaction with the social world and imposed upon individuals by external agents, including both other people and social systems and structures.

Many of the categories that underpin our affiliation with different social groups and our ties with different social roles are culturally constructed ways of classifying people. In his monumental study of the emergence of a distinct working-class identity, E.P. Thompson (1963) highlighted the contribution of both the recognition by working-class people of diverse occupations of their shared interest, and that shared interest set against the interests of other classes. He argued that working-class political consciousness was at least in part imposed by the anxiety of the middle classes about the changing social order, an anxiety that underpins Arnold's (1869) concern with the state of culture. Similarly, although sex is biologically determined, gender roles are at least in part socially constructed: a matter of the values and traditions of particular cultures that find their realisation in norms of social behaviour. Ethnicity is as much about the way in which individuals are perceived within the social system as it is a matter of shared cultural traditions, values and beliefs. Identity is therefore something socially constructed from our interactions within the social world. The *psychological* and *social* components of identity meet in the internalisation of socially constructed ways of classifying people in our sense of self and our sense of place.

Castells (2004: 7) argues: 'Although identities can also be originated from dominant institutions, they become identities only when and if individuals internalise them, and construct their meaning around this internalisation.' The social and personal dimensions of identity are entangled in the complex relationship of our social and psychological being. Identity is therefore by its very nature *complex*, consisting of many interacting aspects that contribute to our sense of self and self-worth: our ties with different social demographic groups on the basis of age, class, race, nationality, gender, sexuality, employment, faith group and so on; the social roles we play, such as familial roles or workplace occupations; our social relationships and the way other people regard us, treat us and interact with us; and the values and beliefs to which we adhere. Out of these aspects of our participation in social life we construct a sense of our place in the world. How identity is manifested may depend on the contexts and social situations in which we find ourselves. People in a sense all *play* at being different versions of themselves, conforming to or transgressing the norms of social behaviour in different contexts.

In the digital age there is a sense in which the security of identity has declined with the changing economic and social structure. Giddens (1991: 169), for example, notes: 'The self in modern society is frail, brittle, fractured, fragmented – such a conception is probably the pre-eminent outlook in current discussions of the self and modernity.' Giddens (ibid.: 21) asserts that 'the reflexivity of modernity actually undermines the certainty of knowledge'. Castells (2004) argued that with the rise of networks, the role of civic society in the construction of identity declines, and the individual construction of identity shifts to an *oppositional* mode in which the self is defined in relation to that which it is not. Some evidence for this idea emerges through the growth of global political action such as the anti-globalisation movement, and through the sedimentation of identity into forms of fundamentalism, of which Castells gives the example of Christian fundamentalism in the USA. Turkle (1996) discussed the way in which online environments allow the opportunity for identity play, leading us to confront aspects of ourselves that we would rather remained hidden. She argues that this can lead to a transformation in our understanding of the nature of our identities in real-life contexts; the construction of identity online forces us to confront the subjective and contested nature of identity in the world. Through these different discourses, some sense persists that technology changes how we understand the nature of identity. This chapter will explore some of those issues, in particular the sedimentation, virtualisation and fragmentation of identity in the digital age.

Disintermediation and digital identity

The digital age presents us with a series of paradoxes. On the one hand identity has become something imposed upon us by the collection and aggregation of personal information of all kinds, but on the other it has also become something more under our control, constructed through our participation in different digital environments. On the one hand identity has become more fixed, sedimented in the records of digital culture, but on the other it has become more fluid, a matter of whom we choose to be in different virtual worlds. And on the one hand identity seems not to matter in the anonymous spaces of digital environments, but on the other it becomes essential to the radical trust through which our participation in digital culture is secured. These dichotomies reflect two very different effects of digital technology on the nature of identity.

Digital technologies have encouraged us to identify the informational value in aspects of our lives from which information was not traditionally extracted, processed, organised or stored. This aggregation of information occurs in relation to both our presence in virtual environments and our presence in the real world. Databases record our transactions in shops, our movements on public transport and around public spaces and our use of governmental and non-governmental services. In law and governance, financial services, education, health, commercial services and retail contexts personal information is routinely collected and used to build personal profiles. The record of our movements in public spaces and on public transport is recorded via smartcards and CCTV. Traces of our online lives are created in our every use of digital information technologies, and multiply through archives, blogs and aggregating services. With the re-emergence of text as a dominant mode of knowledge transmission and communication, our social interactions have lost their ephemeral nature; what we say and to whom we say it have become more persistent. Because of the nature of digital information, records tends to be retained, outliving the contexts for which they were originally collated.[1] A more or less complete record of our social transactions is being created moment by moment. The book of our lives is being written by silent hands every day.

With this aggregation of information, identity increasingly becomes invested in the records of society and culture. Those records tend to replace corporal presence in securing access to services, benefits and rights. Who we are becomes something that is imposed by the apparatus of the state and marketplace, sedimented in the traces and records of our lives. Yet with our use of digital technology we also willingly submit to this sedimentation of our identity, becoming complicit in the proliferation of personal information. Through the use of smartcards, debit and credit cards and loyalty cards we trade personal information for services or greater convenience. When we register with websites or e-mail newsletters we trade privacy for information. We use personalised services despite the fact that those services are often merely a form of targeted marketing. Our identity, who we are, our tastes, our interests, our skills and expertise, have become a kind of currency with which we barter, or an asset that we reinvest in the social system as a means of accessing services and products and facilitating our personal relationships. As a consequence, the market in personal information has proliferated in the digital age. Personal information is aggregated in innumerable sites, from credit referencing agencies and government bodies to marketing agencies, and is used in innumerable ways. Public and private bodies compete over our identity investment, like virtual identity banks in which the commodification of identity is complete.

Yet while identity is in one way more imposed upon us, it is also something we are more complicit in self-consciously constructing in the digital age. Since 1897 an exclusive game has been played out annually by well-connected members of the British establishment. Every year the publishers of *Who's Who* send a short biographical questionnaire to around 30,000 notable individuals. Although some editorial checks are made, *Who's Who* is compiled almost entirely from the responses to these questionnaires. The information contained within it invariably becomes the meat of countless potted biographies and passing enquiries. While lesser people could participate in the game of the construction of a public identity through other publications of record, such as notices of births, deaths and marriages in local and national newspapers and professional journals, those sources never had quite the reach or esteem of *Who's Who*. For most people identity was always something that, while still both self-constructed and imposed, was inseparable from corporeal being. Identity and self were wrapped up in one biological package. But for those individuals represented within the pages of *Who's Who*, what was included in and omitted from the questionnaire returns became the basis of their public profile, proliferating through the various uses to which the reference work was put. Each year there existed an unrivalled opportunity to construct a public profile self-consciously. Unrivalled, that is, until the digital age; because in digital information contexts we all become complicit in the construction of a public identity.

The increasing disintermediation of information and knowledge transmission in the digital age means that virtual environments have become the sites of the construction of identity. Digital technologies have increasingly placed into our hands the power to determine how we are defined within the socio-cultural sphere. Several aspects of this are worth highlighting. In the first place is the construction of a kind of categorical identity related to the norms of social behaviour and social life. This emerges though the kinds of personal profiles that we make public on websites and social networking sites such as Friends Reunited, LinkedIn, Bebo, MySpace and Facebook. In these spaces we willingly share information about our lives, relationships and work, trading anonymity for the convenience and power of social networking. Second are the cultural capital and records of our cultural lives that we willingly submit to social media forums, such as YouTube or Flickr, and post on personal websites and blogs. With the emergence of a more participatory culture, more people are involved in creating and sharing media and cultural objects of different kinds. Related to this are the traces of our interaction that persist in online forums, discussion groups and through blogs, where we make public our opinions, beliefs, fantasies and narratives of our experience. And with the remediation of new media our participation in culture through submissions and contributions to television, radio and publishing also becomes a part of our transactional identity.

The paradox of identity in the digital age reflects the way in which digital technologies have affected both the nature of identity and its socio-cultural function. While the idea of identity is not unanimous with the idea of self, digital technologies contribute to a dislocation of identity from corporeal being. This influence contains three entangled elements: sedimentation, virtualisation and fragmentation. With its sedimentation, identity becomes increasingly disinvested from social processes and reinvested in the persistent *trace* or *record* of those processes. With virtualisation, the sedimentary record or trace of our identities, actions and values becomes disassociated from our corporeal being. With fragmentation, the unity of identity declines.

Sedimentation, virtualisation and fragmentation

Identity sediments in the records of culture identity as the digital traces of our actions and transactions are recorded and stored, and this sedimentary form of identity becomes searchable and machine-processable. In part this represents a continuation of a process under way since industrialisation. The sociologist Max Weber (1946) described the way in which bureaucracy arises from 'administrative rationality' that informs policy and decision-making by retaining a rational approach to problem-solving. Weber traced the rise of the bureaucratic society or state through the influence of the legitimacy invested by procedural and legal authority, and the rise of modern economies, civil politics and a rational political sphere. The bureaucratic state results in the advancement of record-keeping and documentation, and the record is afforded a central role in administration. But as bureaucracy takes hold, bureaucratic decisions replace the authority of the democratically elected officials, such that trust becomes invested in those decisions, leading to a forgoing of democratic accountable governance. The record becomes more important in access to services and rights. As a consequence, it becomes increasingly important to classify, sort and codify individuals to inform administrative decisions. Individuals in their corporeal being become dislocated from the records of their identity. Who we are within the confines of the administrative process becomes less important than how we are contained within the administrative record.

Digital information technologies exacerbate this trend towards administrative rationality, and complete the dislocation of identity from being. But there is something about the nature of this sedimentation of identity in the digital trace of actions and transactions that distinguishes it from Weber's administrative rationality. The site of record-making is no longer restricted to the domain of administrative rationality; consequently, record-making occurs independently of its use within decision-making. In the digital age the making of records has become a by-product of the use of digital technologies in different aspects of our lives. The informational value derived from everyday actions and interactions means that the record is constructed out of the traces of our lives. This trace of our actions and interactions is reincorporated into administrative rationality, as organisations increasingly use information obtained from the cultural sphere to inform administrative decision-making. As a consequence, the kinds of traces that we leave in the digital domain come increasingly to influence our entitlement to services and rights. But the record has also transcended the confines of administrative rationality to influence our social lives and relationships. How these traces contain and reflect our sense of self (or otherwise) plays an increasingly important part in how we understand our own identity.

The sedimentation of identity in the records of culture can lead to the phenomenon of identity poverty, in which a lack of presence in the administrative record prevents individuals accessing rights and services. After the introduction of the 2003 Money Laundering Regulations (SI 2003: 3075) and 2007 Money Laundering Regulation (SI 2007: 2157) in the UK, financial services providers are now required to make further checks on the identity of their customers. Although the forms of documentation confirming identity are not specified, the legislation guidance sets out a number of documents that might be used to confirm identity, including passports, photographic driving licences, local authority council tax bills or utility bills. Unfortunately, there is no necessary reason why any individual should possess any of these forms of identification. Because rights are not licensed, the possession of documentation to prove identity is not a condition of citizenship in the UK. A small group of people are therefore potentially socially excluded from financial services of various kinds, from loans to new bank accounts and even gambling.

The accumulation of information that arises from the use of digital technologies leads in part to a separation of social identity and corporeal being, or to the virtualisation of identity. Identity becomes disinvested from corporeal being and reinvested in digital representations. Power over identity becomes less a matter of power over individuals and more a matter of power over their virtual surrogates. As a result, how we are represented within the cultural sphere becomes more important to our sense of self. On the one hand, because our actions within the new social contexts of digital environments are increasingly coordinated within transactions that involve elements of trust, the sedimentary trace becomes increasingly significant to our ability to contribute to and participate in digital culture. But on the other hand a conferred value becomes attributed to the sites of identity sedimentation. There is a sense in which, in the digital age, presence in the virtual sphere of media and digital communications becomes a part of a self-validation ritual. This is perhaps reflected in the rise of reality television and celebrity culture; when our virtual selves become more important than our real selves, without a presence in the media space we may as well not exist. It is also perhaps reflected in the proliferation of social media, blogs and personal profiles in the early twenty-first century. The digital or media surrogate becomes a way of affirming our own being. Yet this virtualised form of identity is both fragile and brittle, always subject to falsification because of its independence from lived social reality.

Virtualisation completes the separation of identity and corporeal being begun by the sedimentation of the trace of our social lives in the digital record, and leads directly to the fragmentation of identity in digital contexts. With our uses of digital technologies, versions of ourselves tend to proliferate across different virtual environments, from networking sites to virtual worlds. The fragmentation of digital identity is not a fragmentation of the self; who we are in our real lived experience perhaps remains more secure, although, as Turkle (1996) suggests, the digital play of identity perhaps also allows us to recognise the contingent nature of our sense of selves in the real world. But in different digital domains we self-consciously construct versions of ourselves that often bear only a passing resemblance to our real-world selves. And this means that digital identity is itself more fluid, unconstrained by our corporeal being. In digital spaces we can adopt new personas, experimenting with aspects of our personality with which we are uncomfortable or ashamed. We can play at being different people in different environments; participants in virtual worlds often play with identity by gender swapping, creating new personas or adopting social roles that cannot be realised in day-to-day life. While these versions of self are related to the different roles we play and identities we adopt within the social world, they differ in being often entirely independent of one another. We travel under different user-names in different spaces. We slip on different avatars for our visits to virtual worlds. The identity we assume in each of these spaces has little bearing on how we are perceived elsewhere.

In Chapter 7 it was argued that with the stripping of authenticity from the artefacts of digital culture, a form of radical trust underwrites the pragmatic construction of truth and knowledge. This trust is radical because it is invested not in the individual, but in the record or trace of digital transactions. The liquidity and freedom of identity in the digital domain mean that often interactions cannot be validated against corporeal being, but only against virtual being. On the internet, nobody knows you are a dog. This liquid nature of identity in digital information contexts gives opportunities for playful engagement with different aspects of ourselves, but also challenges how we manage digital transactions.

Cairncross (1997: 191–2) has written: 'Paradoxically, the electronic media make it easier for pornographers, hackers, and swindlers to hide behind anonymity while at the same time representing a serious threat to privacy.' The virtualisation and fragmentation of identity undermine the unanimity between records of identity and corporeal being. Terrorists, spam remailers, criminal groups, pornographers and hackers all exploit the liquidity of identity in the digital age to conceal their tracks. With the separation of identity and corporeal being, ensuring that people are who they claim to be becomes increasingly difficult. While there are technological solutions, such as for example digital certificates and digital signatures, by their nature they are susceptible to fraud and misuse.

These new ways of playing with our own sense of self liberate identity from the confines of corporeal being and real-life relationships. We can always escape our digital surrogates, leaving them behind to form new bonds, new relationships and new lives in different skins. But ultimately digital identity is fragile because it is entirely based in a relationship of trust between participants in digital spaces of different kinds, and those relationships of trust are always open to being exploited. The price we pay for being able to become whoever we want to be is uncertainty about who anyone else is.

Identity crisis

The separation of identity from corporeal being that has accompanied its progressive sedimentation, virtualisation and fragmentation is at the heart of some of the most persistent anxieties associated with identity in the digital age. Identity theft, for example, becomes possible because the record or trace of our identity supersedes our corporeal being in access to rights and services. It exemplifies the commodification of identity in the digital age; identity theft is possible because the trace of our identity inscribed in the records of culture has a value independent of our corporeal existence.

One of the most persistent anxieties around identity in the digital age has been the fear of a loss of privacy within the surveillance society. Bell et al. (2004: 153) wrote that 'the advent of cyberspace has raised privacy concerns to unprecedented high levels'. In 2006 the Office of the Information Commissioner published a report on the state of the surveillance society in the UK. The opening lines establish a stark and sombre tone:

> We live in a surveillance society. It is pointless to talk about surveillance society in the future tense. In all the rich countries of the world everyday life is suffused with surveillance encounters, not merely from dawn to dusk but 24/7. (Wood, 2006)

Wood invokes two literary works in his discussion of the surveillance society: George Orwell's *1984* and Franz Kafka's *The Trial.* He also draws on the representation of surveillance in films, referencing *The Net* (1985), *Enemy of the State* (1998) and *Minority Report* (2002). This direct allusion to literary and cinema precursors of the surveillance society is worth briefly dwelling on, as it highlights how when we discuss privacy and surveillance we are often discussing several discrete and independent effects of technology.

The literary work most associated with the threat of an overbearing and intrusive state is George Orwell's *1984* (1949).[2] In it Big Brother watches over the lives of every citizen, penetrating into their homes and their workspaces, documenting everything that happens. Big Brother, the State and the Party all have an ear to private conversations and an eye to private actions. In the twenty-first century, after the decline of communism, the threat of Big Brother, of the intrusive, totalitarian state, seemed to recede. With information flowing increasingly freely between individuals, organisations and countries, the threat to privacy from the state seemed to decline, and increasingly the threat to privacy seemed to come from commercial interests and from crime. But with the emergence of new technology, Big Brother has again become one model of the surveillance society. Through databases and surveillance technology, the state perhaps again has an ear to every conversation and an eye to every action.

1984 was based in part on another work of fiction that provides an alternative metaphor for the surveillance society. In 1944, after reading *We* by the Russian novelist Yevgeny Zamyatin, Orwell wrote: 'I am interested in that kind of book, and even keep making notes for one that may get written sooner or later' (cited by Davison, 1989). *We* was originally banned in Russia, but after its publication in English in 1924 it was republished in translation across Europe. Like *1984* it is a tale foreboding the power of the totalitarian state, but in the novel social control comes not from the intrusion of the state, but from the social pressure to conform that results from the public nature of all relationships, actions and events. It is set in the urban environment of One State where almost everything is constructed out of glass. The lack of privacy in social life underpins the power of the state. Kafka's *The Trial* ([1925] 1937), in which Joseph K. is subjected to a nightmarish world of bureaucracy and social control, provides a third model of the surveillance society. Accused of a crime that is never explained to him, Joseph is drawn into a web of senseless bureaucracy and officialdom, led down paths that never fully resolve themselves.

These three literary works reveal different aspects of the surveillance society, and different kinds of anxiety associated with privacy in the digital age: state surveillance, social surveillance and bureaucratic surveillance. Under state surveillance, the machinery of the state is used to undermine the privacy of the individual; under social surveillance conformity within the social process under conditions of transparent interaction underpin social control; and under bureaucratic surveillance the machinery of administration is dislocated from social structures, leading to an oppressive and restrictive social system. All three have their place in describing the experience of the digital age. With the centralisation of government administrative information processes in, for example, the proposed national identity database and the NHS records database, freedom of action increasingly becomes licensed by central government. The greater use of digital technology in administration has meant that with the dislocation of corporeal being from the record or trace of identity, control over information increasingly comes to determine access to services. But of these three different versions of surveillance and privacy, it is Zamyatin's *We* that perhaps provides the best metaphor for life in the digital age. Castells

(2001: 180) described the internet as 'life in an electronic panopticon', recalling Foucault's (1977) discussion of the panopticon and its relationship to power and control. The digital world is like a state made of glass, where all our actions are carried out in public.

Part of the reason why privacy surveillance has become an issue in the digital age is because of the changes to how we use information. Giddens (1991: 150) notes:

> In the shape of the coding of information or knowledge involved in system reproduction, surveillance mechanisms sever social systems from their external referents at the same time as they permit their extension over wider and wider tracts of time-space.

Digital information is easily duplicable, and gives rise to perfect copies that are virtually cost-free and can be made at a distance. It is easily communicable; we can transmit it over networks, and disseminate it widely or narrowly at little additional cost. Digital information is becoming increasingly cheap to store, particularly in comparison with other media of record. This means in addition that information can be collected and stored without a view as to its potential future use or value. Keeping records of digital information becomes automatic, a by-product of our use of information technologies. Most importantly, digital information can be automatically collected, compiled, collated and processed. Information can be harvested by robots from public sources, automatically classified and stored. And because digital information is machine-processable, it can be retrieved using machine algorithms. Lessig (1999: 151) has written:

> Today's monitoring is different because the technologies of monitoring – their efficiency and their power – are different. In the 1790s the technology was humans; now it is machines. Then the technology noticed only what was different; now it notices any transaction. Then the default was that searchable records were collected; now the default is that all monitoring produces searchable records.

As a consequence surveillance can take place *routinely*, with neither the value of the information recovered nor the use to which it may be put being predetermined. Lessig (ibid.: 143) discussed two aspects of surveillance in the digital age: the 'part of anyone's life that is *monitored*, and [the] part that can be *searched*'. Surveillance becomes systematic when the part of anyone's life that can be monitored is routinely and systematically transformed into records that can be searched. This is increasingly the case with the use of digital technologies in various social contexts: mobile phone records; global satellite positioning devices; smartcards for public transport use and building access, and so on.

But the nature of technology and digital information is not sufficient to explain the threat posed by surveillance. With the shift in the structure of advanced capitalist societies away from industry and towards services, implicit in Bell's (1974) post-industrialism, Castells's (2000) network society or Schiller's (1976; 1986) commodification of information, information itself has become more central to the economy. As a result more information is produced, disseminated and exchanged at a higher value. Information becomes critical to market differentiation, and a viable commodity in its own right. This is explicit in the rise of information service providers, from content aggregators to business and commercial information providers and credit referencing agencies. Globalisation has led to a decentralisation of commerce, and this has meant that more companies are relying on a distributed network structure. The commodification of identity through the proliferation of personal information in the digital age underpins how through sedimentation, fragmentation and virtualisation, identity and being have become divorced.

Notes

1. The persistence of personal data is of course impacted by national and international data protection law and treaties.
2. The allusion to *1984* in discussion of privacy and the surveillance society is common. See for example Cairncross (1997); Castells (2004); Keen (2007).

9

Memory

The digital age seems like an era that has both forgotten it own past and neglected its own future. While on the one hand it is difficult to imagine a more complete record of everyday life than we are creating moment by moment in our use of digital technologies, on the other hand our impression on recorded history threatens to be slight. This chapter explores how digital technologies affect the cultural memory. It will consider three aspects of that question: the preservation of digital records, the nature of the digital archive and how digital information technologies are changing our understanding of the past. Memory is the site of the active shaping and filtering of experience; to remember is also to forget and to recall is also to exclude. The cultural memory is not a static record of the past but is actively created in the present. How we understand our past and future is therefore also a matter of how we situate ourselves in the present. This chapter argues that the anxiety about a loss of cultural memory reflects not only tension about our relationship with the past, but also tensions about the role of digital information technologies in our lives in the present and the foreseeable future.

Digital preservation

Digital preservation relates to the active and ongoing management of digital resources over time. It concerns two kinds of digital artefacts. Non-native artefacts are those cultural objects that have been subject to digitisation. They may include written records, artwork, music and audio, film, video and material cultural objects. Native digital artefacts are those cultural objects that were originally created digitally. They may include e-mails, digital photographs, software, computer games, television programmes, digital artworks, e-journals and e-books, websites, database contents, digital recordings and so on. Much of the information created in the modern age is born digital and dies digital. Of these we can identify two types: those distributed and disseminated via material media, such as CDs, DVDs and computer software; and those distributed and disseminated via digital networks. Increasingly, we are moving to digital distribution of digital content. Computer games, music, software, e-books, e-journals, websites, television programmes and digital artworks are all now routinely disseminated in this way to varying degrees. This digitally distributed content often has a fragile material existence, dependent on its continued use. As more of the cultural memory is moved to the digital domain, ensuring that these records remain accessible in the future becomes a more pressing concern.

The problem of the preservation of digital culture is exemplified by two widely cited cases. In the 1980s the National Archive in Washington state, USA, transferred around 250,000 documents and images on to laser video disks. By 2002 it was unclear whether the information was still recoverable, because the required software and hardware were no longer available (Stille, 2002). In 1986 the BBC marked the 900th anniversary of the Domesday Book with a project to create a digital record of life in the late twentieth century. It employed cutting-edge technology, a conjunction of the new digital video disk and existing BBC micros, standard educational computers in the UK at the time. The digital Domesday Book would provide an interactive resource for use in educational contexts, combining documentation, video clips, sound recording and photographs in an innovative multimedia package. Within a few short years it was obsolete; CD ROMs and DVDs had replaced digital video disks, and working BBC micros were few and far between. While the original Domesday Book had survived for over 900 years, its digital equivalent was all but unreadable in only 15 (McKie and Thorpe, 2002; Wheatley, 2004). In the digital age, the future of the past is under threat. Stille (2002: 300) observes:

> One of the great ironies of the information age is that, while the late twentieth century will undoubtedly have recorded more data than any other period in history, it will also almost certainly have lost more information than any previous era.

The digital age has seen an exponential growth in the amount of information created, used and stored (Conway, 1996; von Baeyer, 2003). As more native digital information is created and disseminated, a greater part of our culture is documented only in the digital domain. Much of this content is of only marginal historical interest, but the sheer volume of information in the digital age makes its selection and filtering for the purposes of archiving and preservation more problematic. Old strategies that depended on the cultural sifting of discourse and knowledge through the apparatus of publishing and administration, such as for example legal deposit, break down in an age where information proliferates in every aspect of daily life.

In addition digital information tends to be highly ephemeral, existing only briefly before being destroyed. The value of paper as a medium of storage is exhausted in the paper record, but because most digital media are rewritable, they have a continued value independent of the information inscribed on them. When digital content falls out of use, the storage medium in which it is housed is often reused for other content. Web server space is reallocated for new services. Magnetic drive space is reallocated for new content. As a result, digital content lacks *persistence*: the material record will continue to exist until it is destroyed, but by contrast the digital record is usually destroyed unless it is consciously preserved. The rewritable nature of most digital media also means that digital information tends to be highly mutable, changing to meet the needs of its producers and users. Digital records lack the finality of the paper record or printed work. This mutability creates problems for preservation: when the information on a particular resource is constantly changing, the idea of a definitive final document that can be secured for the future breaks down; all information becomes a work in progress. One approach to addressing this mutability, used by both the independent Internet Archive[1] and the UK Web Archiving Consortium, has been to take sequential snapshots of digital content at given points in time. However, this neither guarantees to capture a full picture of the constantly mutating information landscape nor resolves which versions of particular resources are significant and why. If anything, it threatens to add to the problems posed for the preservation of digital culture by the proliferation of information.

But the dilemma of preservation does not merely reflect the changing status of information in culture; it also arises from the intrinsic volatility of both digital technologies and digital storage media. Conway (1996) notes: 'Our capacity to record information has increased exponentially over time while the longevity of the media used to store the information has reduced equivalently.' There appears to be an inverse correlation between the density and longevity of media of record. Vellum barely degrades over time if stored correctly, but is bulky, difficult to manage and a low-density medium. Paper is more usable, higher density and durable if stored under the right conditions, but its acid content leads to its own degradation. The higher acid content of the lower-quality paper used in mass-circulation newspaper and paperback publishing means that these artefacts degrade more quickly. Microfilm and microfiche are higher density, and still a preferred archival medium, but deteriorate over a period of between 100 and 300 years. Digital media tend to be very high in density but low in stability. Optical disks degrade because of a reaction between the surface and foil layers. Magnetic media are vulnerable to electromagnetic interference. Most digital media have a potential life of less than 25 years. This intrinsic volatility means that without intervention the records of the contemporary age will deteriorate more quickly than those of any time in recorded history.

In addition records have become over time increasingly technologically dependent. All record-making relies on technologies of different kinds; both the preparation of vellum in manuscript culture and the printing presses of the modern age are forms of technology. But in both these cases the technological intervention in the making of records occurs prior to the point of their use within culture. As a consequence the value and meaning of the artefact remain transparent at the point of its consumption; information is encoded in a transparent way, allowing unmediated access to its meaning and value. Throughout the twentieth century record-making has increasingly relied on technologies of different kinds, and the encoding of information in material media has become gradually more opaque. In principle information stored on microfiche and microfilm remains recoverable with only a strong light source and a means of magnification. The perforations of paper tape and punched cards are more opaque, but if the encoding format is understood then in principle the data remain recoverable without technological mediation. However, magnetic and optical media are entirely dependent on technological intervention. Not only are they designed only to be machine-readable, but the information they encode often only makes sense within a particular computing context. The value of a recorded computer program is inseparable from its operating environment; the value of many computer files is inseparable from the programs with which they were created.[2]

Unfortunately, there is a very rapid cycle of innovation and obsolescence for computing hardware, software and encoding formats of all kinds. As new technologies are developed, old technologies are quickly abandoned. Although this does not absolutely prohibit the recovery of obsolete digital records, it creates considerable practical barriers. Firstly, the recovery of obsolete digital information requires a considerable metaknowledge of hardware, software and encoding formats. Secondly, it may also require a considerable investment in recreating or refurbishing the technologies of the past. Thirdly, because of the opaque nature of digital media, the value of the record may not be apparent prior to its recovery. This creates a Catch 22 dilemma: knowing whether the digital records of the past are worth reading depends on first recovering those records, but investing in their recovery depends on knowing their value.

For a variety of reasons to do with the nature of digital technology, it is unlikely that we will develop in the near future digital media that are as stable as the paper record. This means that for the records of digital culture to survive into the future, we become committed to an active form of preservation where information is constantly migrated between platforms, media and encoding formats. But active preservation poses its own problems that limit the potential survival of information in the digital age. It is resource-intensive, which means we can commit ourselves to preserving only a limited selection of the available digital record. This implies difficult questions about the basis on which that selection is made and what values it represents. In addition, while we can ensure the short-term preservation of digital artefacts through this approach, it is impossible to guarantee that future societies will share our values and continue these endeavours. A digital record not actively preserved will become unreadable within perhaps only two or three decades, and lost to culture. A short hiatus in the chain of preservation will do irreparable damage to the cultural record.

These issues add up to a very big problem for the future of the past. Not only is it impossible to be certain that much of the digital information we are currently producing will be accessible in the future, but it appears likely that it will not be so. We are living in an age that is producing ever more information and data, but which is leaving ever less of an impression on the historic record.

The digital dark ages

Does the problem of digital preservation matter? On the face of it this seems like a straightforward question: the historical record is such a valuable source of knowledge and understanding that it is difficult to accept that in our rush towards a digital future the loss of that record can be of no material consequence. But does the digital age really threaten a loss of the historical record, or merely a loss of the archive? The two are not quite the same. In this chapter it will be argued that the anxiety of digital preservation reflects a conflict of narratives that converge on the continuing role of the archive in securing the preservation of the artefacts of digital culture. The idea of the archive, as an ideal and not an institution, becomes less secure in an age when the stability and fixedness of recorded information are themselves placed under question. But the idea of the archive perhaps also reflects the values of an age when knowledge was invested in only a very few sites of creation and transmission. This chapter will argue that the tension between the stable cultural record and the unstable digital record contains not only an expression of the changing role of the record-making itself, but also a conflict between two versions of history and two ways of framing the past and its relationship to the present.

The uncertain future of the past is often described as auguring a 'digital dark age'.[3] This phrase captures both the idea of a hiatus in recorded knowledge and its potentially devastating consequences for knowledge and learning by drawing a parallel between the late medieval period and the digital age. It is worth briefly exploring this idea, as it exposes some of the tacit anxieties that lie behind the dilemma of digital preservation. The early medieval period became known as the dark ages largely in reflection of the perceived decline of knowledge, learning and culture after the classical era, particularly the loss of classical learning in the Aristotelian tradition. The metaphor partly represents a backwards construction from the idea of the Enlightenment; the apparent darkness of the early medieval period is in part merely the shadow cast by the brilliance of the modern period. But 'dark' also represents a marked linguistic form (cf. Chandler, 2002: 114) incorporating tacit value judgements about the comparative states of knowledge and culture in the two periods. The opposition of darkness and light functions to valorise the modern age at the expense of the medieval. It is now generally recognised that the early Middle Ages were not as brutal and unlearned as once assumed. What survives of Anglo-Saxon culture, for example, suggests a strong literary tradition, a concentration of scholarship in certain geographic areas and a sophisticated documentary culture, exemplified by the work of Bede and Alfred the Great. The impression of a decline in learning and knowledge is created in part only by the paucity of documentary evidence surviving from the period. The metaphor of the dark ages therefore functions to valorise Enlightenment culture in three ways: by constructing an opposition between the medieval and modern; by imposing values smuggled into that opposition in the idea of darkness and light; and by conflating the surviving documentary record with the state of culture and learning. As a metaphor it therefore tells us more about the values of the period in which it was formed than about the state of knowledge during the time it is supposed to represent.

The 'digital dark age' functions in a similar way, and incorporates a number of assumptions about the progress of knowledge and its relationship to the documentary record. In the first place, in the use of the marked linguistic form the metaphor encloses a tacit opposition between Enlightenment rationalism and the digital age. Secondly, this opposition implies comparative levels of culture, knowledge and learning; the light of the modern period is fast fading in the digital age. Thirdly, it conflates the continuing security of documentary records with the continuing security of knowledge, learning and culture. The real metaphorical force of the phrase is therefore invested in the idea that digital technologies threaten a loss of learning and the death of the Enlightenment age; the digital dark age is not just a way of describing the threatened caesura in the documentary record, but of moving from that threatened caesura to an assertion about the state of digital culture. For example, Deegan and Tanner (2002) wrote:

> The Gutenberg printing revolution led Europe out of the Dark Ages – the loss of knowledge of the learning of the ancient Greeks and Romans. The digital revolution may land us in an age even darker if urgent action is not taken.

As it stands, this statement is historically inaccurate. The recovery of classical learning in Western Europe occurred throughout the high and late Middle Ages, largely as a result of the intellectual exchange between Islamic and Christian cultures. Printing had almost no impact on that process, and there is a danger of overstating the importance of the print revolution on the status of knowledge before the Enlightenment. There is perhaps an irony in the cavalier treatment of historical progress underpinning this expression of a perceived threat to the future of the past. But the accuracy of the statement is in many ways neither here nor there, because while it purports to reveal some parallel with the past, it really only functions to assert a particular view of the present. The assertion converges on the role of technology in not only securing a certain level of knowledge and culture, but also in bringing about its decline. It is, after all, printing that emerges as the prime agent of socio-cultural betterment in Deegan and Tanner's caricature of the Enlightenment, and the replacement of printing and printed works by digital surrogates that emerges as the prime agent of its decline in the modern age. The concern with knowledge and the historic record is conflated with an anxiety that digital technologies undermine the hard-won gains of the printing revolution.

The metaphor of a digital dark age is powerful and alluring because it is so suggestive. But the parallel between the early medieval period and the digital age is entirely false, perpetuating not only discredited accounts of early medieval culture and the transition to the Renaissance and later the Enlightenment, but also by association an unfounded pessimism about the state of digital culture. In this it both contains and reflects a broader narrative of socio-cultural decline. But of perhaps more interest is the way in which it encloses anxieties about the relationship between the entangled triplets of culture, knowledge and learning, and their dependence on the dominant mode of information reproduction and dissemination. In part this may reflect the role of disintermediation in how we understand the experience of the digital age. With increased disintermediation, control over narratives about the past invested in archive records and libraries declines. The archive itself, not as an institution but as an ideal, loses its central place in the idea of the past at the moment it loses its mediating role in the authentication of knowledge. But it also reflects the role of digital technologies in undermining the privileged place of the printed work. While printing dragged us into what Burrow (1982) has called 'continuous culture' by stabilising the documentary record, digital technologies threaten to return us to an 'intermittent culture' where we are condemned to rediscovering existing knowledge in each generation.

What remains unarticulated is that digital technologies principally threaten neither the documentary record nor even the idea of objective knowledge, but how we frame and understand the past, and by extension our own place within the sweep of history. By destabilising both writing and the written record, digital technologies undermine the security of a knowable past. Implicit in this is a conflict between different versions of history, historical objectivity and historical method. And it is in this conflict that the anxiety over digital preservation is really located.

Versions of history

The historian Keith Jenkins (1991: 7) notes that 'the past and history are different things', adding that they 'float free of each other; they are ages and miles apart'. While the objective occurrence of past realities is only rarely seriously doubted, the possibility of recovering an objective account of those events within contemporary discourse is less certain. Jenkins highlights the gulf between the kinds of truths that are possible within the discourse of history and the past reality that they seek to contain and reflect. Most historians subscribe at least in principle to the idea of a knowable past. Indeed, it is against this idea that the practice of history is legitimised. Alun Munslow (2006: 3) has written:

> Modernist or 'proper' history bases its claims to legitimacy as a discipline by discovering the meaning of a past reality: a meaning that is enduring and can be described or represented faithfully by the suitably distanced historian.

The idea of a knowable past is what separates history from other kinds of discourses; it is what makes the pursuit of history more than just a kind of story-telling, and distinguishes historical narrative from myths. The historical narrative is legitimised inasmuch as it contains and reflects the objective truths and meanings of past realities. There is in this idea an important distinction between the objective past reality and the subjective historical narrative. Because the historical record is necessarily incomplete and the historical narrative involves the historian in further filtering and selection, historical narratives cannot by themselves be regarded as objective accounts of a past reality. The objective truth of that reality always belongs to the past. But through disinterested critical distance, such narratives do aspire to objectivity, and are legitimised against the past events that they seek to contain: historical narratives are true to the degree that they reflect and contain past experiences. The historical process therefore converges on the knowable past through the discourse of history.

Through the latter part of the twentieth century this assumption about the possibility of a knowable past was challenged by a new school of historians. The post-modern turn in historiography challenged two key assumptions of modernist history: the aspiration of critical distance and disinterest in the construction of objectively dispassionate historical narratives, and the intrinsic relationship between the discourse of history and the experience of past realities that it sought to contain and describe. Foucault (1980, 1991a) argued that what comes to be regarded as legitimate knowledge is governed by the play of power through discourse, which functions to filter the social reality through particular forms of knowledge. The documentary record on which the discourse of history was built was itself only a partial representation of past realities, valorising certain dominant perspectives and accounts and marginalising others. Hayden White (1978) drew on literary theory in exploring the tropes of historical discourse. More recently, the post-modernist historian Keith Jenkins analysed the tacit assumptions underpinning historical practice. He described history as merely 'one of a series of discourses about the world' that, while not creating the world, appropriate it and give it meaning (Jenkins, 1991: 69). Jenkins argued that historical narratives are simply ways of constructing an understanding about the past and its continuing relevance in the present; as a consequence, 'history in the main is what historians make' (ibid.: 31).

Modernist and post-modernist historiography divide around the relationship between the discourse of history and the past that it seeks to represent and contain. They turn on the question of whether the past reality is objectively knowable in the present. The idea of the ongoing presence of past realities and experiences mediated through social and cultural discourses is a human universal. Both oral and manuscript cultures possess their own historicity rooted in myths, folktales, genealogies and cultural practices such as ancestor worship. Ovid's *Metamorphosis* ([c. 2–5 AD] 1986), the *Anglo-Saxon Chronicle* ([c. 892–1154] 1961), Bede's *Historia ecclesiastica gentis Anglorum* ([c. 731] 1999) and the medieval chronicle of Jean Froissart ([1322–1400] 2001) all contain versions of the past. But these versions of history do not converge on the idea of a knowable, recoverable past in the way claimed by modernist historiography. That idea of a knowable past secured against the documentary record of past realities emerges through the modern age. Munslow (2006) has linked its emergence with the Enlightenment ideal of objective knowledge, noting that the aspirations of critical distance and disinterest mirror the ideals of Enlightenment rationalism. But while the idea of recoverable knowledge about past realities may have been formalised only after the Enlightenment, it took root in the growing uses of writing in the early modern period, particularly after the advent of print. In English, the transition between mythical and historical discourse can be traced quite precisely. One of the first uses of 'history' in something like a modern sense occurs in John Gower's *Confessio Amantis*, written in the 1390s (Gower, [c. 1390] 1900, IV: 660). Gower's idea of *histoire* did not imply either veracity towards past realities or the aspiration to document past experiences, but was merely a framework for hanging moral truths 'essampled of these olde wyse' (ibid., Prologue: 7). The use of *history* in relation to a continuous methodical record of events and circumstances begins with Caxton in 1485 (OED, 1989). Although the idea of an objective past was beginning to germinate in late manuscript culture, it took root under conditions of print reproduction.

Printing did not determine the nature of history in the modern age, but it did provide part of the foundations on which the modernist historiography could be built. The investiture of the written record with a particular kind of authority under conditions of print reproduction informed the idea of a knowable past that became central to modernist historiography. It is not, of course, the case that only printed artefacts make up that documentary record, but printing changed the values associated with the uses of writing of all kinds. The fixedness of the printed work imbued the written record with the finality and authenticity that were preconditions of the idea of history as an objective account of past realities. The written record was a repository for the experiences, events and perspectives of a people that can be passed down through time and used as a basis to construct knowledge of historical events and circumstances. As a result the knowable past became largely synonymous with the documentary record filtered through historical analysis, and subject to the critical disinterest of the modernist historian. But by separating oral and literate cultures and making literacy a condition of participation in discourse, printing also acted to marginalise other versions of history that emerge through myth, story-telling and oral culture. What was present in the documentary record was only a fragment of the lived reality of past ages. Which experiences were represented in that record depended very much on control over the apparatus of record-making. The conflation of the past with a documentary past therefore tended to marginalise the experiences of those people without access to the apparatus of knowledge creation and transmission, and valorise the experiences of those who held power over this apparatus.

Historical scholarship is inseparable from the uses of writing in two ways. Firstly, it involves the creation of narratives that traditionally, and still almost universally, are written. Secondly, the study of history is largely a study of a *documentary* history that is contained in the written artefacts of culture. The two uses of writing in historical practice are inseparable; the historical narrative becomes a part of the documentary record and historical narratives therefore become reincorporated into the historical process. Post-modernist historiography challenged the assumptions underpinning both uses of writing within the historical process. The past was not to be found in the detritus of documentary culture because past realities are not fully realised within the historical record, and the historical narrative does not contain past realities because the historians cannot be divorced from the historical narratives for which they are responsible. It is notable that this challenge to traditional notions of history occurred at precisely that point when the authenticity of the written record and the authority of writing themselves were placed under question by the electronic communication media of the twentieth century. As a result of the secondary literacy of electronic communications technologies (Ong, 1982), and later as a result of digital information technology, the centrality, stability and finalised nature of writing came to be things that could no longer be assumed. Indeed, post-modernist theory encloses a self-conscious articulation of the challenges of the mass media and digital computing. The writers who became key influences on the formation of post-modern historiography enacted in their work the tension between the old technologies of print and the new technologies of electronic and digital communication.[4] By drawing on the post-modernist critique, the tension between writing and record became incorporated into the new historiography.

Memory in the digital age

At the beginning of this chapter it was noted that memory is the site of the active shaping and filtering of the past. By stabilising the ontology of writing, printing perhaps encouraged the impression of a dead and static historical record to which we can merely add. Digital technologies, on the other hand, bring us to a new reconciliation with the idea of memory and a tacit recognition that the past is always filtered through the preoccupations of the present. This forces us to approach the relationship between history and culture in a new light. Brand (1999) has argued:

> If raw data can be kept accessible as well as stored, history will become a different discipline, closer to a science, because it can use marketers' data-mining techniques to detect patterns hidden in the data. You could fast-forward history, tease out correlated trends, zoom in on particular moments.

While this view reflects a reductive and naïve notion of the nature of history and its relationship to the records of culture, it also reflects a kind of culmination of the modernist desire to trace the experience of past realities through its documentary residue. But if digital technologies hold out the promise of the fulfilment of that desire, they also highlight how imperfectly realised it will always be within the discourse of history. No matter how comprehensive our archives, the documentary record can never be complete, because the *experience* of lived past realities and the records of culture cannot be synonymous. Historical narratives are therefore denied finality by resort to either critical distance and disinterest or the complete cultural record. They must always be selective and partial, reflecting the values of the age in which they are created as much as the values of the age they seek to contain and describe. The selectivity of memory is critical to its cultural function, lest, as with Sterne's eponymous *Tristram Shandy* ([1759] 1992), the enterprise of representing reality overtakes and subsumes reality itself. It is in this sense, and only in this sense, that digital technologies threaten a loss of the cultural memory; not a loss of knowledge but of only the impression of certainty embedded in the apparent finality of the written record.

The idea of the digital dark ages captures this anxiety of a slow awakening from the dream of a knowable past into the dilemma of historical uncertainty. And this itself is a frightening idea, shattering the ontological security of our historical situatedness. It is in the tension between a documentary history and the possibility of a knowable past that both the anxieties of digital preservation and the perceived threat of technology to the continuation of the cultural memory are really contained. The value of the archive is in part secured against the testimony provided by the material history of documents, but as records are shifted to the digital domain they are stripped of their material presence, denying them intrinsic authenticity. Preserving the instructions for recreating records implies a different set of values, assumptions and conventions from preserving the material record itself. The possibility of silent intervention in the artefacts of digital culture means that the authenticity of the archive is less secure; the digital archive may well be a place of illusion and deceit. By undermining the stability of the historical record, digital technologies also undermine the role of the archive. While printing in part acted to stabilise our conception of the past by stabilising the written record, digital technologies threaten to destabilise the record, cutting the past loose from its cultural moorings.

In the dilemma of digital preservation is a tacit inversion of the relationship between the historical record and the process of making records. The social and cultural practice of making records is not motivated by a preoccupation with the knowable past, and the value of the record to our understanding of past realities plays little part in that practice. The idea of a knowable past informed by critical objectivity is on the contrary a consequence of a particular cultural practice of record-making, and informed by the structural qualities of the technology which makes that practice possible. The investiture of the written record with a particular kind of authority lies behind the value of the archive; because recorded history is such a rich source of information about the past, captured within a single medium, archives and libraries became the centre of its preservation and storage. But as well as being centres for the preservation of memory, archives and libraries also become actors in the authentication and validation of particular historical accounts (cf. Tredinnick, 2006). What is incorporated into the library and archive forms the basis of the knowable past. But what is incorporated into the library and archive also perpetuates degrees of presence of different lived experiences within the historical record.

The archive's role in concentrating the idea of the cultural memory in a documentary trace and in authenticating certain kinds of experience leads to an overemphasis on its role in maintaining the future of memory. Decisions taken in the present only marginally affect the future of knowledge and memory; the information that makes up the historical record has survived largely because it became actively valued and used, rather than because of abstract decisions taken about its worth. The manuscripts that survive from before the age of print tend to be those that were most widely copied, disseminated and read. Books printed in larger numbers from the early modern period are those more likely to survive today. Printing helped to stabilise the idea of a documentary history by stabilising individual texts and making possible preservation strategies to secure their survival. But the archive, like the library of Alexandria, is atypical in this process of cultural propagation, an explicit aspiration to petrify documentary culture in something like a complete and final form. In the impossibility of its realisation that aspiration is naïve, but it reflects a particular mode of record-making characteristic of the modern age. When the idea of the past becomes invested in the documentary record, other narratives filtered through oral discourse and tradition fall out of memory. The petrifying of the cultural memory in the archive becomes not only possible, but also critical to its survival. With so much of the cultural memory concentrated into so few sites of record, those sites become individually more critical to the survival of the cultural memory. Memory becomes itself concentrated on the archive. The structures of the modern age that mediated knowledge creation and dissemination locked the archive into a particular relationship with the past reality that it preserved.

In the digital age the relationship between the nature of history and the cultural record is changing. The making of records has increasingly become a side-effect of the use of digital technologies. By encouraging us to identify the informational value contained in every aspect of our social lives, digital technologies create traces of almost all our actions and interactions, etched into the memory banks of our machines. As a consequence more people participate in the creation of the cultural record than at any other point in history. This represents a very different form of record-making from that of the modern age. Information is no longer filtered before being entered into the record, but is now filtered at the point of its consumption and use. The volume of recorded information has as a result proliferated beyond measure, and the *documentary* record of digital culture threatens to overwhelm the cultural memory. Preservation strategies break down with the inundation of digital artefacts; under the weight of digital culture it becomes impossible to select individually those records that will survive to represent us in the future.

The decline of the archive, not as an institution but as an ideal, reflects the futility of traditional approaches to maintaining the cultural record in an age of disintermediation and decentralisation of knowledge creation, dissemination and transmission. By continuing to insist on a documentary history difficult to maintain in an age when we produce too many documents which reflect too many divergent perspectives and which have an ephemeral nature of their own, we undermine the objectivity of a documentary history. And under the weight of digital culture that aspiration to preserve through selection implies new ethical questions. The proliferation of records means that digital preservation becomes a more explicitly *politically* situated practice. Because archival decisions are informed by tacit values that will tend to valorise some outlooks at the expense of others, the selection of information for preservation becomes an overtly politically situated practice acting to legitimise some versions of history and truth. These politically charged questions explicitly extend the scope and role of the archive.

An example of these ethical dilemmas emerges through the way in which digital preservation tends to memorialise ephemeral social exchanges. Bassett and O'Riordan (2002) discussed two dominant metaphors for the World Wide Web that impact on the ethical dimension of research. On the one hand the web is a social space in which ideas and viewpoints are shared and our online lives lived. But on the other hand it is also a kind of text, in which ideas and opinions are sedimented into fixed expressions. These two metaphors situate the idea of the web quite differently. What occurs in a social space is ephemeral, lasting for only the duration of the interaction. But text is durable, designed to communicate across time; the text intentionally reflects the possibility of its own future presence. The debate around digital archiving treats digital content as equivalent to the formal texts of the age of print. But the nature of the textual medium is changing in the digital age. The digital world is both a social sphere and a site of record. Digital preservation therefore confronts us with the ethical issues created by memorialising the ephemeral in the digital archive. By transforming an ephemeral social space into a site of record, digital technologies blur the boundaries between private lives and documentary history. This forces us to view the role of the continuing archive in a new, ethically poised light.

The new historicity

Recognising that history is not something sedimented in the centres of record, a static trace of the past, but something created and constructed in the present out of our relationship with the past relieves some of the anxiety of digital preservation. The continuing presence of the past is constructed in our continuing engagement with its trace. Kuny (1998) has written:

> We are, to my mind, living in the midst of digital Dark Ages; consequently, much as monks of times past, it falls to librarians and archivists to hold to the tradition which reveres history and the published heritage of our times.

This is a romantic ideal, but the state of knowledge in the digital age is not analogous to that in the early medieval period, when so much of the documentary record was concentrated in only a relatively few centres, artefacts and books. Information saturates every aspect of our lives. We are surrounded by our history; not a dry historical archive, but a living history created in our everyday concerns, cares and interests. The duplicability of digital information and the proliferation of copies through its cycle of use have meant that while the media of storage may be more volatile in the digital age, much information is persistent, outlasting the original contexts for which it was created. The digital documentary record will not be preserved in central repositories, but through our exchange of information and knowledge. The real digital archive is not concentrated in formal mechanisms for legal deposit and preservation, but saturates the entire social network. By sharing information we become part of a living archive.

With this recognition comes also a new historicity of digital culture. Rather than becoming more distant from us, the past has become more integrated into our everyday social lives. The documentary record is increasing available for everybody to use and share. The role of the historian in creating the historical narrative out of the detritus of documentary culture is supplemented by the role of individuals in making their own sense of the past. The knowable past invested in the records of libraries and archives is supplemented by a kind of social historical process. This is perhaps most explicit in the case of genealogy; for a variety of reasons[5] the digitisation of genealogical records is more complete than it is for other aspects of documentary history. With the more ready availability of genealogical information, the popularity of family history has grown. As more of our historic record is put online, and in more accessible forms, perhaps history will become less the preserve of historians and more the preserve of society. The idea of history perhaps changes: less a dead record and more an active engagement with the past out of which each of us makes our own sense, and through dialogue in the digital sphere we come together to a shared sense of our relationship with the past. The discourse of history will perhaps meet culture halfway in an assimilation of the documentary past into the memorial histories of social discourse.

The irony is that the distributed creation, dissemination and storage of information and knowledge in the digital age, far from representing a threat to the future of the cultural memory, are possibly the most secure preservation strategy of all. The central archive is always vulnerable to disruption. Collections are lost precisely because they are gathered in one place. Distributed information is by its very nature persistent; it tends to outlive the contexts for which it was originally created. As soon as information is disseminated via a distributed network, copies begin to proliferate and live their own lives. If that information is useful, interesting, titillating or shocking, then it is disseminated more widely. Distributed information tends to survive on the basis that its value is widely recognised within the social and cultural flux. Its survival is not dependent on individual assessments of its future value or worth. Questions remain about the mutability and authenticity of the digital record, but these are questions that relate not to the security of knowledge and information but to the epistemology of writing. The survival of the record emerges through a pragmatic constructivist mode of knowledge in which the entire social process is complicit in the authentication of knowledge.

Notes

1. Available at www.archive.org/.
2. Emulation has become as a consequence increasingly a part of digital preservation strategies. See Granger (2000); Thibodeau (2002).
3. See for example Brand (1999); Deegan and Tanner (2002); Kuny (1998).
4. Johnson (1997: 46) observed that Derrida's thinking was inspired by 'the *practice* of new information and communications technologies developed in the post-war period' and that 'it is the presence and pervasiveness of this new ambient technology which makes possible the grammatological enquiry into the essence of writing'. Lyotard (1984) believed that the status of knowledge could not remain unchanged in the face of new technologies. Baudrillard (1994) argued that electronic communications technologies divorce content from meaning.
5. The most important is probably the Mormon project to digitise records of births, deaths and marriages. Another factor is the widespread interest in genealogy within the USA, where the use of the web is somewhat ahead of the rest of the world.

Epilogue: culture and tradition

During its composition, this became a book about more than anything the process of change in the digital age: how we situate ourselves within a mutating cultural tradition, how we cope with the constantly shifting terrain of culture and how we manage the new challenges posed by the emerging cultural forms and social spaces of the digital age. Change is of course not a particularly original theme; the mutability of experience in the face of time is an enduring preoccupation. Throughout this book it has been argued that how we explain and contain the experience of change within the cultural sphere also influences how we experience that change. The kinds of narratives that we tell about our experiences change the way in which we confront the digital world.

In Chapter 5 it was suggested that cultural creativity pertains to the forging of a dialogue with tradition. That is to say that tradition remains alive through the way in which it is reincorporated into the lived culture. New cultural forms, values and practices have an advantage over tradition in not being encumbered by history. But it is also the case that when we compare new cultural forms, values and practices with the cultural tradition, we are not comparing like with like. Emergent forms and practices take time to uncover their potential, delimit their own boundaries, realise their potential and mature. And time has a sifting effect, weeding out the false starts and mistakes of the past. All emergent cultural forms and practices at the time of their appearance therefore appear unrefined. The novel was not immediately the dominant literary form. Film and television took time to find out what they do best. How digital culture is experienced in this ongoing moment of its gradual emergence, eager and green, is perhaps unrepresentative of its future potential.

There are several remaining issues that need touching on briefly at the end of this book. The first is a question of narratives. In Chapter 3 it was suggested that all accounts of change resolve to narrative formations, because they project a synchronic account of development structured out of linear sequential events. It could be argued that this book is just another kind of narrative, just another way of projecting a selective account of change on to the whole social experience. It tells the story of how change is experienced in the moment of its occurrence as a conflict between value systems and experience. It tells a series of stories about the relationship between culture and technology. This is indeed the case. This book does not try to escape the fact that it is just one story of change. It does not aspire to closure and finality. It does not pretend to be the last word on digital culture. It differs from some other accounts, perhaps, not only in the kinds of stories that it tells but in acknowledging that they are just stories whose value is measured not in how well they capture the reality of the social system, but in how well they reflect an experience of culture in the digital age. This is not to suggest that narratives lack truth, but to recognise that truths are merely what we make of them.

More critically, there is a kind of performative contradiction at the heart of this book. One persistent theme with which it has engaged is the rise of a more participatory culture, but as a printed work it denies the reader any real participation in its own meaning. It is therefore abstract from many of the changes on which it passes comment and over which it passes judgement. Through the qualities of its material form it pretends to finality and closure and not openness and play. It is in its own terms the last word on its own meaning. I do not believe this is necessarily a good thing; it is just in the nature of the printed work. Similarly, it has been argued that the mutability of digital textuality undermines the values of the print tradition, but as a printed work this book aspires to fixedness and finality. It participates in an original authorial act against which its value and meaning are measured. Again, this is just in the nature of the printed work. I do not believe that traditional forms lose their value in a digital age, merely that their value shifts by some degree. However, there is one effect of print reproduction to which I would like to draw attention at the end of this book. By setting ideas in a fixed form, the printed book can give the impression that those ideas are themselves finalised. As a printed work this book may pretend to finality and closure, but I do not myself regard the arguments within it as final and closed. The last chapter of socio-cultural change always remains unwritten.

References

Literature

Aldiss, Brian (1973) *Billion Year Spree: The History of Science Fiction*. London: Weidenfeld & Nicholson.

Althusser, Louis ([1971] 2006) 'Ideology and ideological state apparatuses (notes towards an investigation)', in Durham, Meedakshi Gigi and Kellner, Douglas (eds) *Media and Cultural Studies Keyworks; revised edition*. Malden and Oxford: Blackwell Publishing, pp. 79–87.

Anderson, Nate (2006) 'Tim Berners-Lee on Web 2.0: nobody even knows what it means'; available at: *http://arstechnica.com/news.ars/post/20060901-7650.html* (accessed: 19 December 2007).

Anderson, P.W. (1972) 'More is different', *Science*, 177(4047): 393–6.

Andretta, Susie (2004) *Information Literacy: A Practitioner's Guide*. Oxford: Chandos Publishing.

Anglo-Saxon Chronicle ([c.892–1154] 1961) *The Anglo-Saxon Chronicle: a revised translation; edited by Dorothy Whitelock with David C. Douglas and Susie I. Tucker; introduction by Dorothy Whitelock*. London: Eyre & Spottiswoode.

Arnold, Matthew (1869) *Culture and Anarchy: An Essay in Political and Social Criticism*. London: Smith, Elder & Co.

Asimov, Isaac (1950) *I Robot*. New York: Gnome Press.

Atwood, Margaret (1985) *The Handmaid's Tale*. Toronto: McClelland and Stewart.

Austin, John Langshaw (1976) *How to Do Things with Words*. London: Oxford University Press.

Balkin, J.M. (1998) *Cultural Software: A Theory of Ideology*. New Haven and London: Yale University Press.

Barker, Chris (2002) *Making Sense of Cultural Studies: Central Problems and Critical Debates*. London: Sage Publications.

Barry, P. (2002) *Beginning Theory: An Introduction to Literary and Cultural Theory*. Manchester and New York: Manchester University Press.

Barthes, Roland ([1957] 1972) *Mythologies; selected and translated from the French by Annette Lavers*. London: Jonathan Cape.

Barthes, Roland ([1968] 1977) 'The death of the author', in Barthes, Roland *Image Music Text: essays selected and translated by Stephen Heath*. London: Fontana, pp. 142–8.

Bassett, E.H. and O'Riordan, Kathleen (2002) 'Ethics of internet research: contesting the human subjects research model', *Ethics and Information Technology*, 4(3): 233–47.

Baudrillard, Jean (1994) *Simulacra and Simulation; translated by Sheila Faria Glaser*. Michigan: University of Michigan Press.

Baugh, Albert C. and Cable, Thomas (1993) *A History of the English Language*, 4th edn. London: Routledge.

BBC (1999) 'Pagans celebrate as numbers soar'; available at: *http://news.bbc.co.uk/1/hi/uk/500484.stm* (accessed: 18 October 2007).

BBC (2006) 'Britain "worse than 20 years ago"'; available at: *http://news.bbc.co.uk/1/hi/uk/5310016.stm* (accessed: 19 September 2007).

BBC (2007) 'Most say UK is in "moral decline"'; available at: *http://news.bbc.co.uk/1/hi/uk/6982805.stm* (accessed: 19 September 2007).

Bede ([c. 731] 1999) *The Ecclesiastical History of the English People; new edited edition*. Oxford: Oxford University Press.

Bell, Daniel (1974) *The Coming Post-Industrial Society: A Venture in Social Forecasting*. London: Heinemann Education.

Bell, David, Loader, Brian, Pleace, Nicholas and Schuler, Douglas (2004) *Cyberculture: The Key Concepts*. London and New York: Routledge.

Benjamin, Walter ([1936] 1970) 'The work of art in the age of mechanical reproduction', in Benjamin, Walter *Illuminations; edited by Hannah Arendt, translated by Harry Zorn*. London: Jonathan Cape, pp. 211–44.

Bennett, Andrew and Royle, Nicholas (1999) *An Introduction to Literature, Criticism and Theory*, 2nd edn. London: Prentice Hall.

Blackmore, Susan (1999) *The Meme Machine*. Oxford and New York: Oxford University Press.

Blair, Tony (2007) 'Our nation's future – public life'; available at: *www.number10.gov.uk/output/Page11923.asp* (accessed: 20 October 2007).

Bolter, Jay David and Grusin, Richard (2000) *Remediation: Understanding New Media*. Cambridge, MA, and London: MIT Press.

Borges, Jorge Luis (1962) 'The library of Babel', in Borges, Jorge Luis *Labyrinths: Selected Stories and Other Writings; edited by Donald A. Yates and James E. Irby*. New York: New Directions Publishing.

Brand, Stewart (1999) 'Escaping the digital dark age', *Library Journal*, 124(2): 46–8.

Brewer, Derek (1982) 'The social context of medieval English literature', in Ford, Boris (ed.) *The New Pelican Guide to English Literature: Medieval Literature*. London: Penguin, pp. 15–42.

Bromley, Catherine (2007) 'Can Britain close the digital divide?', in Park, Alison, Curtice, John, Thomson, Katarina, Phillips, Miranda and Johnson, Mark (eds) *British Social Attitudes; 23rd Report, Perspectives on a Changing Society*. London: Sage Publications, pp. 72–95.

Brown, Dan (2004) *The Da Vinci Code*. London and New York: Bantam Press.

Bruner, Jerome (1986) *Actual Minds, Possible Worlds*. Cambridge, MA, and London: Harvard University Press.

Buckland, Michael (1991) 'Information as thing', *Journal of the American Society for Information Science*, 42(5): 351–60.

Buckland, Michael (1997) 'What is a document?', *Journal of the American Society for Information Science*, 48(9): 804–9.

Buckland, Michael (1998) 'What is a digital document?', *Document Numérique*, 2(2): 221–30.

Burns, Enid (2007) 'Top ten search engine providers, August'; available at: *http://searchenginewatch.com/showPage.html?page=3627122* (accessed: 20 October 2007).

Burrow, J.A. (1982) *Medieval Writers and Their Work: Middle English Literature and Its Background 1100–1500*. Oxford: Oxford University Press.

Bush, Vannevar (1945) 'As we may think', *Atlantic Monthly*, 176(1): 101–8.

Cairncross, Frances (1997) *The Death of Distance: How the Communications Revolution Will Change Our Lives*. London: Orion Business Books.

Carruthers, Mary J. (1990) *The Book of Memory: A Study of Memory in Medieval Culture*. Cambridge: Cambridge University Press.

Castells, Manuel (2000) *The Information Age: Economy, Society and Culture Volume I: The Rise of the Network Society*, 2nd edn. Malden, MA, Oxford and Victoria: Blackwell Publishing.

Castells, Manuel (2001) *The Internet Galaxy: Reflections of the Internet, Business, and Society*. Oxford and New York: Oxford University Press.

Castells, Manuel (2003) *The Information Age: Economy, Society and Culture Volume II: The Power of Identity*, 2nd edn. Malden, MA, Oxford and Victoria: Blackwell Publishing.

Castells, Manuel (2004) *The Information Age: Economy, Society and Culture Volume III: End of Millennium*, 2nd edn. Malden, MA, Oxford and Victoria: Blackwell Publishing.

Chandler, Daniel (2002) *Semiotics: The Basics*. London and New York: Routledge.

Chaucer, Geoffrey ([c. 1382] 1988a) 'Troilus and Criseyde', in Benson, Larry D. (ed.) *The Riverside Chaucer; new edition*. Oxford and New York: Oxford University Press.

Chaucer, Geoffrey ([c. 1385] 1988b) 'Chaucers wordes unto Adam, his own scriveyn', in Benson, Larry D. (ed.) *The Riverside Chaucer; new edition*. Oxford and New York: Oxford University Press.

Chomsky, Noam (1957) *Syntactic Structures*. The Hague: Mouton.

Cicero, Marcus Tullius ([63 BC] 1974) *Selected Works; translated by M. Grant*. London and New York: Penguin.

Clanchy, M.T. (1993) *From Memory to Written Record: England 1066–1307*, 2nd edn. Oxford: Blackwell Publishing.

Clarke, Arthur C. (1945) 'Extra-terrestrial relays: can rocket stations give world-wide radio coverage?', *Wireless World*, October: 305–8; available at: *www.lsi.usp.br/~rbianchi/clarke/ACC.ETRelays.html* (accessed: 19 September 2007).

Clarke, Arthur C. (1973) *Profiles of the Future: An Enquiry into the Limits of Possibility; revised edition*. London: Pan Books.

COED (2006) *Concise Oxford English Dictionary*, 11th revised edn. Oxford and New York: Oxford University Press.

Connolly, Ray (2007) 'How we lost the magic of childhood', *The Daily Mail*, 3 April: 13.

Conway, Paul (1996) 'Preservation in the digital world', Council of Library and Information Resources; available at: *www.clir.org/pubs/reports/conway2/* (accessed: 3 May 2006).

Crystal, David (2001) *Language and the Internet*. Cambridge: Cambridge University Press.

Cullen, Rowena (2001) 'Addressing the digital divide', *Online Information Review*, 25(5): 311–20.

Czarniawska, Barbara (2004) *Narratives in Social Science Research*. London: Sage Publications.

Davison, Peter (1989) 'A note on the text', in Orwell, George *1984*. London and New York: Penguin.

Dawkins, Richard (1976) *The Selfish Gene*. Oxford and New York: Oxford University Press.

Deegan, Marilyn and Tanner, Simon (2002) 'The digital dark ages', *Library and Information Update*, 1(2): 41–2.

Descartes, René ([1641] 1962) *The Meditations and Selection from the Principles of René Descartes*. La Salle: Open Court.

Dick, Philip K. (1972) *Do Androids Dream of Electric Sheep?* London: Grafton.

Disch, Thomas M. ([1986] 1991) 'Introduction', in Dick, Philip K. *We Can Remember It For You Wholesale; The Collected Stories of Philip K. Dick V. 5*. London: Grafton.

Duffy, Eamon (1992) *The Stripping of the Altars: Traditional Religion in England 1400–1580*. New Haven and London: Yale University Press.

Dutton, William H. and Helsper, Helen J. (2007) *The Internet in Britain 2007*. Oxford: Oxford Internet Institute.

Dvorak, John C. (2006) 'Web 2.0 baloney'; available at: *www.pcmag.com/article2/0,1895,1931858,00.asp* (accessed: 7 August 2007).

Eagleton, Terry (1984) *The Function of Criticism*. London: Verso.

Eagleton, Terry (1996) *Literary Theory, an Introduction*, 2nd edn. Oxford and Malden, MA: Blackwell Publishing.

Eagleton, Terry (2000) *The Idea of Culture*. London: Blackwell Publishing.

Eisenstein, Elizabeth ([1983] 2007) 'The rise of the reading public', in Crowley, David and Heyer, Paul (eds) *Communications in History: Technology, Culture, Society*. Boston, MA: Pearson Education, pp. 95–103.

Eisenstein, Elizabeth (2005) *The Printing Revolution in Early Modern Europe*, 2nd edn. Cambridge and New York: Cambridge University Press.

Electoral Commission (2005) *Election 2005 Turnout: How Many, Who and Why*; available at: *www.electoralcommission.org.uk/files/dms/Election2005turnoutFINAL_18826-13874__E__N__S__W__.pdf* (accessed: 18 October 2007).

Eliot, T.S. (1948) *Notes Towards the Definition of Culture*. London: Faber & Faber.

Engels, Frederick ([1890] 2006) 'Letter to Joseph Bloch', in Storey, John (ed.) *Cultural Theory and Popular Culture: A Reader*, 3rd edn. Harlow: Pearson Education.

Feather, John (1988) *A History of British Publishing*. London and New York: Routledge.

Feather, John (2004) *The Information Society: A Study of Continuity and Change*. London: Facet Publishing.

Feuerbach, Ludwig ([1841] 1957) *The Essence of Christianity; translated from the German by George Eliot*. New York: Harper & Row.

Fischer, Steven Roger (1999) *A History of Language*. London: Reaktion Books.

Fischer, Steven Roger (2000) *A History of Writing*. London: Reaktion Books.

Fischer, Steven Roger (2003) *A History of Reading*. London: Reaktion Books.

Flanagan, Andrew J. and Metzger, Miriam J. (2007) 'The role of site features, user attributes, and information verification behaviours in the perceived credibility of web-based information', *New Media and Society*, 9(2): 319–42.

Fogg, B.J. (2003) 'Prominence-interpretation theory: explaining how people assess credibility', in *Proceedings of CHI 2003, April 5–10, 2003, F. Lauderdale, Florida, USA*. New York: Association for Computer Machiners, pp. 722–3.

Foucault, Michel (1967) *Madness and Civilisation: A History of Insanity in the Age of Reason; translated by Richard Howard*. London: Tavistock Publications.

Foucault, Michel (1970) *The Order of Things: An Archaeology of the Human Sciences*. London: Tavistock Publications.

Foucault, Michel (1972) *The Archaeology of Knowledge: translated by A.M. Sheridan Smith*. London: Tavistock Publications.

Foucault, Michel (1977) *Discipline and Punish: The Birth of the Prison; translated from the French by Alan Sheridan*. London: Allen Lane.

Foucault, Michel (1979) *The History of Sexuality, Vol. 1: Introduction; translated from the French by Robert Hurley*. London: Allen Lane.

Foucault, Michel (1980) *Power/Knowledge: Selected Interviews and Other Writings 1972–1977; edited by Colin Gordon*. London: Longman.

Foucault, Michel (1984a) *The History of Sexuality, Vol. 2: The Use of Pleasure; translated from the French by Robert Hurley*. Harmondsworth: Penguin.

Foucault, Michel (1984b) *The History of Sexuality, Vol. 3: The Care of the Self; translated from the French by Robert Hurley*. Harmondsworth: Penguin.

Foucault, Michel ([1991a] 1992) 'Truth and power', in Rabinow, Paul *The Foucault Reader: An Introduction to Foucault's Thought*. London and New York: Penguin, pp. 51–75.

Foucault, Michel ([1991b] 1992) 'What is an author', in Rabinow, Paul *The Foucault Reader: An Introduction to Foucault's Thought*. London and New York: Penguin, pp. 101–20.

Freud, Sigmund ([1930] 2002) *Civilization and Its Discontents; translated by David McLintock*. London: Penguin.

Froissart, Jean ([1322–1400] 2001) *Froissart's Chronicles; translated and edited by John Jolliffe*. London and New York: Penguin.

Fukuyama, Francis (1989) 'The end of history?', *The National Interest*, 16 (Summer): 3–18.

Fukuyama, Francis (1992) *The End of History and the Last Man*. London: Penguin.

Gardner, Howard (1987) *The Mind's New Science: A History of the Cognitive Revolution; with a new epilogue by the author*. London: HarperCollins.

Genette, Gérard (1997) *Paratexts: Thresholds of Interpretation; translated by Jane E. Lewin; foreword by Richard Macksey*. Cambridge: Cambridge University Press.

Gibson, Owen (2007a) 'BBC apologises to Queen over claim she threw a tantrum during photo-shoot', *The Guardian*, 13 July, p. 5.

Gibson, Owen (2007b) 'Film-maker blames ITV for Alzheimers "death" furore', *The Guardian*, 2 August, p. 6.

Gibson, William (1984) *Neuromancer*. London: Victor Gollancz.

Gibson, William (1986) 'Johnny Mnemonic', in Gibson, William *Burning Chrome*. London: Victor Gollancz.

Giddens, Anthony (1991) *Modernity and Self-Identity: Self and Society in the Late Modern Age*. Cambridge: Polity Press.

Gleick, James (1999) *Faster: The Acceleration of Just About Everything*. London: Little, Brown.

Google (2007) 'Google milestones'; available at: *www.google.com/intl/en/corporate/history.html* (accessed: 2 October 2007).

Gower, John ([c. 1390] 1900) *Confessio Amantis*, in Macauley, G.C. *The English Works of John Gower*. Oxford: Early English Text Society.

Granger, Stuart (2000) 'Emulation as a digital preservation strategy', *D-Lib Magazine*, 6(10); available at: *http://webdoc.sub.gwdg.de/edoc/aw/d-lib/dlib/october00/granger/10granger.html* (accessed: 26 September 2007).

Hall, Stuart ([1980] 1986) 'Culture studies, two paradigms', in Collins, Richard, Curran, James, Garnham, Nicholas, Scannell, Paddy, Schlesinger, Philip and Sparks, Colin (eds) *Media, Culture and Society: A Critical Reader*. London: Sage Publications, pp. 33–48.

Hall, Stuart ([1980] 2006) 'Encoding/decoding', in Durham, Meedakshi Gigi and Kellner, Douglas (eds) *Media and Cultural Studies Keyworks*. Malden and Oxford: Blackwell Publishing, pp. 163–73.

Harland, Richard (1987) *Superstructuralism: The Philosophy of Structuralism and Post-Structuralism*. London: Methuen.

Harris, Roy (2001) *Rethinking Writing*. London and New York: Continuum.

Heath, Anthony, Martin, Jean and Gabriella, Elgenius (2007) 'Who do we think we are: the decline of traditional social identities', in Park, Alison, Curtice, John, Thomson, Katarina, Phillips, Miranda and Johnson, Mark (eds) *British Social Attitudes; 23rd Report, Perspectives on a Changing Society*. London: Sage Publications, pp. 1–33.

Hesse, Hermann ([1943] 2000) *The Glass Bead Game*. London: Random House.

Hobbes, Thomas ([1651] 1994) *Leviathan; introduced by Kenneth Minogue*. London: J.M. Dent.

Hoggart, Richard (1957) *The Uses of Literacy: Aspects of Working-Class Life with Special Reference to Publications and Entertainments*. London: Chatto & Windus.

Hoggart, Richard (1991) 'The abuses of literacy', *Guardian Weekly*, 7 July, p. 22.

Holmwood, Leigh (2007) 'Refund offer by C4 over Richard and Judy quiz', *The Guardian*, 20 February, p. 4.

Horkheimer, Max and Adorno, Theodor W. ([1944] 2006) 'The culture industry: enlightenment as mass deception', in Durham, Meedakshi Gigi and Kellner, Douglas (eds) *Media and Cultural Studies Keyworks; revised edition*. Malden and Oxford: Blackwell Publishing, pp. 41–72.

Hutton, Lord (2004) *Report of the Inquiry into the Circumstances Surrounding the Death of Dr David Kelly C.M.G.*; available at: *www.the-hutton-inquiry.org.uk/content/report/index.htm* (accessed: 20 October 2007).

Huxley, Aldous (1932) *Brave New World*. London: Chatto & Windus.

Jameson, Fredric (1991) *Postmodernism, or, the Cultural Critique of Late Capitalism*. London: Verso.

Jenkins, Henry ([2003] 2006) 'Quentin Tarantino's *Star Wars*? Digital cinema, media convergence and participatory culture', in Durham, Meedakshi Gigi and Kellner, Douglas (eds) *Media and Cultural Studies Keyworks; revised edition*. Malden and Oxford: Blackwell Publishing, pp. 549–76.

Jenkins, Keith (1991) *Re-thinking History*. London and New York: Routledge.

Johnson, Christopher (1997) *Derrida: The Scene of Writing*. London: Phoenix.

Johnson, Steven (2001) *Emergence: The Connected Lives of Ants, Brains, Cities and Software*. London: Allen Lane.

Justice, Stephen (1996) *Writing and Rebellion: England in 1381*. Berkeley and London: University of California Press.

Kafka, Franz ([1916] 1961) *Metamorphosis*, in Kafka, Franz *Metamorphosis and Other Stories; translated by Willa and Edwin Muir*. London and New York: Penguin.

Kafka, Franz ([1925] 1937) *The Trial; translated by Willa and Edwin Muir*. London: Victor Gollancz.

Keen, Andrew (2007) *The Cult of the Amateur: How Today's Internet is Killing Our Culture and Assaulting Our Economy*. London and Boston, MA: Nicholas Brealey Publishing.

Keen, Maurice (1990) *English Society in the Later Middle Ages 1348–1500*. London: Penguin.

Kristeva, Julia (1980) *Desire in Language: A Semiotic Approach to Literature and Art*. New York: Columbia University Press.

Kroeber, Alfred Louis and Kluckhohn, Clyde (1952) *Culture: A Critical Review of Concepts and Definitions*. New York: Vintage Books.

Kuny, Terry (1998) 'The digital dark ages? Challenges in the preservation of electronic information', *International Preservation News*, 17 (May): 8–13.

Larrain, Jorge (1979) *The Concept of Ideology*. London: Hutchinson & Co.

Leavis, F.R. ([1930] 2006) 'Mass civilisation and minority culture', in Storey, John (ed.) *Cultural Theory and Popular Culture: A Reader*, 3rd edn. Harlow: Pearson Education.

Leavis, F.R. (1952) 'Literary criticism and philosophy', in Leavis, F.R. *The Common Pursuit*. London: Chatto & Windus, pp. 211–22.

Lessig, Lawrence (1999) *Code: And Other Laws of Cyberspace*. New York: Basic Books.

Lévi-Strauss, Claude (1966) *The Savage Mind*. London: Weidenfeld & Nicholson.

Lévi-Strauss, Claude (1968) *Structural Anthropology; translated from the French by Claire Jacobson and Brooke Grundfest Schoepf*. London: Allen Lane.

Lévi-Strauss, Claude (1969) *The Raw and the Cooked; translated from the French by John and Doreen Weightman*. New York: Harper & Row.

Lewin, Roger (1999) *Complexity: Life at the Edge of Chaos*, 2nd edn. Chicago: University of Chicago Press.

Lyotard, Jean-François (1984) *The Postmodern Condition: A Report on Knowledge*. Manchester: University of Manchester Press.

Malpas, Simon (2005) *The Postmodern*. London and New York: Routledge.

Manguel, Alberto (1996) *A History of Reading*. London: HarperCollins.

Manson, Steven M. (2001) 'Simplifying complexity: a review of complexity theory', *Geoform*, 32: 405–14.

Marx, Karl ([1859] 1968) 'A contribution to the critique of political economy', in *Karl Marx and Fredrick Engels Selected Works in One Volume*. London: Lawrence and Wishart.

McDonald, Ronan (2007) *The Death of the Critic*. London: Continuum.

McKie, Robin and Thorpe, Vanessa (2002) 'Digital Domesday Book lasts 15 years not 1,000', *The Observer*, 3 March, p. 7.

McLuhan, Marshall (1962) *The Gutenberg Galaxy: The Making of Typographic Man*. London: Routledge & Kegan Paul.

McLuhan, Marshall (1964) *Understanding Media: The Extensions of Man*. London: Routledge & Kegan Paul.

Metzger, Miriam J., Flanagan, Andrew J., Eyal, Keren, Lemus, Daisy R. and McCann, Robert M. (2003) 'Credibility for the 21st century: integrating perspectives on source, message and media credibility in the contemporary media environment', in Kalbfleisch, Pamela J. (ed.) *Communication Yearbook 27*. Mahwah, NJ: Lawrence Erlbaum Associates.

Milton, John ([1667] 1968) *Paradise Lost; edited by Christopher Ricks*. London and New York: Penguin Classics.

Morson, Gary Saul (1994) *Narrative and Freedom: The Shadows of Time*. New Haven and London: Yale University Press.

Mumford, Lewis ([1947] 2007) 'The invention of printing', in Crowley, David and Heyer, Paul (eds) *Communications in History: Technology, Culture, Society*. Boston, MA: Pearson Education, pp. 91–5.

Munslow, Alun (2006) *The Routledge Companion to Historical Studies*, 2nd edn. London and New York: Routledge.

Negroponte, Nicholas (2005) 'The $100 laptop: the next two billion people go digital', 24th Annual Morgenthau Memorial Lecture; available at: *www.cceia.org/resources/publications/morgenthau/5283.html* (accessed: 19 October 2007).

Nelson, Theodor Holm (2000) 'Xanalogical structure, needed now more than ever: parallel documents, deep links to content, deep versioning and deep re-use'; available at: *http://xanadu.com.au/ted/XUsurvey/xuDation.html* (accessed: 5 May 2007).

OED (1989) *The Oxford English Dictionary: second edition; prepared by J.A. Simpson and E.S.C. Weiner*. Oxford: Clarendon Press.

Ong, Walter J. (1982) *Orality and Literacy: The Technologizing of the Word*. London: Methuen & Co.

ONS (2003) '390,000 Jedis there are'; available at: *www.statistics.gov.uk/cci/nugget.asp?id=297* (accessed: 18 October 2007).

ONS (2007a) 'Union membership'; available at: *www.statistics.gov.uk/cci/nugget.asp?id=4* (accessed: 18 October 2007).

ONS (2007b) 'Focus on the digital age'; available at: *www.statistics.gov.uk/focuson/digitalage/* (accessed: 18 October 2007).

O'Reilly, Tim (2005) 'What is Web 2.0?'; available at: *www.oreillynet.com/pub/a/oreilly/tim/news/2005/09/30/what-is-Web-20.html?page=1* (accessed: 20 October 2007).

Orwell, George (1949) *1984: A Novel.* London: Secker & Warburg.

Ovid ([c. 2–5 AD] 1986) *Metamorphosis; a new translation by A.D. Melville.* Oxford and New York: Oxford University Press.

Paolillo, John, Pimienta, Daniel, Prado, Daniel, Mikami, Yoshiki and Fantognan, Xavier (2005) *Measuring Linguistic Diversity on the Internet.* Paris: UNESCO; available at: *http://unesdoc.unesco.org/images/0014/001421/142186e.pdf* (accessed: 18 October 2007).

Pinker, Steven (1994) *The Language Instinct: The New Science of Language and Mind.* London: Allen Lane.

Platt, Charles (1995) 'Interactive entertainment: who writes it? Who reads it? Who needs it?', *Wired*, 3(9): 59–63.

Popper, Karl (1957) *The Poverty of Historicism.* London and New York: Routledge & Kegan Paul.

Postman, Neil (1992) *Technopoly: The Surrender of Culture to Technology.* New York: Knopf.

Power Enquiry (2006) *Power to the People: The Report of Power, an Independent Commission into Britain's Democracy*; available at: *www.makeitanissue.org.uk/Power%20to%20the%20People.pdf* (accessed: 18 October 2007).

Ritzer, George (1996) *The McDonaldization of Society.* London: Sage Publications.

Roberts, Genevieve (2006) 'Childhood is being ruined warn experts', *The Independent*, 13 September, p. 12.

Robertson, D.W. (1962) *Preface to Chaucer: Studies in Medieval Perspectives.* London: Oxford University Press.

Robinson, James (2007) 'Upset Ant and Dec give profits to charity after phone-in scandal', *The Observer*, 21 October, p. 11.

Rosenberg, Scott (2007) 'The blog haters have barely any idea what they are raging against', *The Guardian*, 29 August, p. 27.

Schiller, Herbert I. (1976) *Communication and Cultural Domination.* White Plains and New York: Internationals Arts and Sciences Press.

Schiller, Herbert I. (1986) *Information and the Crisis Economy.* Oxford and New York: Oxford University Press.

Scott, C.P. (1921) *A Hundred Years*; available at: *www.guardian.co.uk/newsroom/story/0,11718,850815,00.html* (accessed: 16 October 2007).

Shaw, Russell (2005) 'Web 2.0? It doesn't exist'; available at: *http://blogs.zdnet.com/ip-telephony/?p=805* (accessed: 7 August 2007).

Shelley, Mary ([1885] 1992) *Frankenstein or A Modern Prometheus.* London and New York: Penguin Classics.

Starn, Randolph (1975) 'Meaning-levels in the theme of historical decline', *History and Theory: Studies in the Philosophy of History*, 14(1): 1–31.

Steinberg, S.H. (1974) *Five Hundred Years of Printing; with a foreword by Beatrice Warde.* Harmondsworth: Penguin.

Sterne, Laurence ([1759] 1992) *The Life and Opinions of Tristram Shandy, Gentleman; edited by Melvyn New.* London: Macmillan Education.

Stille, Alexander (2002) *The Future of the Past: How the Information Age Threatens to Destroy Our Cultural Heritage.* London, Basingstoke and Oxford: Picador.

Storey, John (1997) *An Introduction to Cultural Theory and Popular Culture*, 2nd edn. London: Longman.

Taylor, Mark C. (2001) *The Moment of Complexity: Emerging Network Culture.* Chicago and London: University of Chicago Press.

The Daily Telegraph (2006) 'Lost childhoods', *The Daily Telegraph*, 12 September, p. 23.

Thibodeau, Kenneth (2002) 'Overview of technological approaches to digital preservation and challenges in coming years', in *Proceedings of the State of Digital Preservation: An International Perspective, Washington, April 24–25 2002*, Council of Library and Information Resources; available at: *www.clir.org/pubs/reports/pub107/pub107.pdf* (accessed: 26 September 2007).

Thompson, Bill (2007) 'Daily reality of net censorship'; available at: *http://news.bbc.co.uk/1/hi/technology/7047592.stm* (accessed: 20 October 2007).

Thompson, E.P. (1961a) 'The long revolution I', *New Left Review*, 9: 24–33.

Thompson, E.P. (1961b) 'The long revolution II', *New Left Review*, 10: 34–39.

Thompson, E.P. (1963) *The Making of the English Working Class.* London: Victor Gollancz.

Thrift, Nigel (1999) 'The place of complexity', *Theory, Culture and Society*, 16(3): 31–69.

Toffler, Alvin (1970) *Future Shock.* London: Bodley Head.

Toffler, Alvin (1980) *The Third Wave.* London: William Collins & Sons.

Tredinnick, Luke (2006) *Digital Information Contexts: Theoretical Approaches to Understanding Digital Information.* Oxford: Chandos Publishing.

Turing, Alan ([1950] 2004) 'Computing machinery and intelligence', in Copeland, Jack B. (ed.) *The Essential Turing: The Ideas that Gave Birth to the Computer Age.* Oxford and New York: Oxford University Press, pp. 441–64.

Turing, Alan ([1951a] 2004) 'Intelligent machinery, a heretical theory', in Copeland, Jack B. (ed.) *The Essential Turing: The Ideas that Gave Birth to the Computer Age.* Oxford and New York: Oxford University Press, pp. 472–5.

Turing, Alan ([1951b] 2004) 'Can digital computers think?', in Copeland, Jack B. (ed.) *The Essential Turing: The Ideas that Gave Birth to the Computer Age.* Oxford and New York: Oxford University Press, pp. 482–6.

Turkle, Sherry (1996) *Life on the Screen: Identity in the Age of the Internet.* London: Weidenfeld & Nicholson.

Turner, Graeme (1990) *British Cultural Studies: An Introduction.* London and New York: Routledge.

Urry, John (2005) 'The complexity turn', *Theory, Culture and Society,* 22(5): 1–14.

UNESCO (2001) *UNESCO Universal Declaration on Cultural Diversity*; available at: *www.unesco.org/education/imld_2002/unversal_decla.shtml* (accessed: 17 January 2007).

von Baeyer, Hans Cristian (2003) *Information: The New Language of Science.* London: Weidenfeld & Nicholson.

Vonnegut, Kurt (1953) *Player Piano.* London: Macmillan.

Vonnegut, Kurt (1985) *Galapagos.* London: Jonathan Cape.

Waldrop, Mitchell M. (1992) *Complexity: The Emerging Science at the Edge of Order and Chaos.* New York: Simon & Schuster.

Weber, Max (1946) 'Bureaucracy', in Gerth, Hans and Wright Mills, C. (eds) *Max Weber.* Oxford and New York: Oxford University Press.

Weiser, Mark (1991) 'The computer for the 21st century', *Scientific American*, 265 (September): 94–104; available at: *www.ubiq.com/hypertext/weiser/SciAmDraft3.html* (accessed: 25 October 2007).

Wells, H.G. (1895) *The Time Machine: An Invention.* London: W. Heinemann.

Wells, H.G. (1937) 'The idea of a permanent world encyclopaedia', *Encyclopédie Française*, August; available at: *http://sherlock.berkeley.edu/wells/world_brain.html* (accessed: 7 May 2006).

Wells, H.G. (1938) *The Invisible Man*. Harmondsworth: Penguin.

Wheatley, Paul (2004) 'Digital preservation and the BBC Domesday'; available at: *http://aic.stanford.edu/sg/emg/library/pdf/wheatley/Wheatley-EMG2004.pdf* (accessed: 25 September 2007).

White, Hayden (1978) *Tropics of Discourse: Essays in Cultural Criticism*. Baltimore and London: Johns Hopkins University Press.

White, Hayden (1979) 'Michel Foucault', in Sturrock, John (ed.) *Structuralist and Since: From Lévi-Strauss to Derrida*. Oxford and New York: Oxford University Press, pp. 81–115.

Williams, Raymond (1958) *Culture and Society 1780–1950*. London: Chatto & Windus.

Williams, Raymond (1961) *The Long Revolution*. London: Chatto & Windus.

Williams, Raymond (1974) *Television: Technology and Cultural Form*. London: Fontana.

Williams, Raymond (1977) *Marxism and Literature*. Oxford: Oxford University Press.

Williams, Raymond (1980) 'Base and superstructure in Marxist cultural theory', in Williams, R. *Problems in Materialism and Culture: Selected Essays*. London: Verso, pp. 31–49.

Williams, Raymond (1981) *Culture*. Glasgow: Fontana.

Williams, Raymond (1983) *Keywords: A Vocabulary of Culture and Society; revised and expanded edition*. London: Flamingo Press.

Wolfreys, Julian (1998) *Deconstruction: Derrida*. London: Macmillan.

Wood, David Murakami (ed.) (2006) 'A report on the surveillance society for the Information Commissioner by the Surveillance Studies Network'; available at: *www.ico.gov.uk/upload/documents/library/data_protection/practical_application/surveillance_society_full_report_2006.pdf* (accessed: 13 October 2007).

Wyndham, John (1960) *The Trouble with Lichen*. London: Michael Joseph.

Zamyatin, Yevgeny ([1924] 1972) *We; translated by Mirra Ginsburg*. New York: Avon Books.

Other media

2001: *A Space Odyssey* (1968) Film, directed by Stanley Kubrick. UK/USA: MGM.

The Beatles (1995) 'Free as a Bird', in The Beatles *Anthology I* (audio recording on CD). UK: Apple Corp/EMI Records.

Bebo (2006) Website; available at: *www.bebo.com* (accessed: 20 October 2007).

Being John Malkovich (1999) Film, directed by Spike Jonze. USA: Gramercy Pictures.

Blade Runner (1982) Film, directed by Ridley Scott. USA: Blade Runner Partnership.

Blake's Seven (1978–1981) Television series. UK: BBC.

Children of Men (2006) Film, directed by Alfonso Cuarón. Japan/UK/USA: Universal Pictures.

Cole, Natalie (2000) 'Unforgettable', in Nat King Cole *The Unforgettable Nat King Cole* (audio recording on CD). USA: Capitol.

The Crow (1994) Film, directed by Alex Proyas. USA: Crowvision.

Dark Star (1974) Film, directed by John Carpenter. USA: Jack H. Harris Enterprises.

Digg (2004) Website; available at: *www.digg.com* (accessed: 20 October 2007).

Dr. Strangelove or: How I Learned to Stop Worrying and Love the Bomb (1964) Film, directed by Stanley Kubrick. UK: Hawk Films.

Enemy of the State (1998) Film, directed by Tony Scott. USA: Touchstone Pictures.

Eternal Sunshine of the Spotless Mind (2004) Film, directed by Michel Gondry. USA: Anonymous Content.

Facebook (2004) Website; available at: *www.facebook.com* (accessed: 20 October 2007).

Flickr (2002) Website; available at: *www.flickr.com* (accessed: 20 October 2007).

Friends Reunited (2000) Website; available at: *www.friendsreunited.co.uk* (accessed: 20 October 2007).

Gattaca (1998) Film, directed by Andrew Niccol. USA: Columbia Pictures.

George Lucas in Love (1999) Short film, directed by Joe Nussbaum. USA: Quality Filmed Entertainment.

Give a Few Bob (2007) Television advertisement, created by Alan Curson and Caroline Jenkins. UK: The Communications Agency.

The Island (2005) Film, directed by Michael Bay. USA: Dreamworks SKG.

The Jedi Who Loved Me (2000) Short film, directed by Henry Burrows and Adam Lopez. UK: Foiled Productions; available at: *www.foiled.co.uk/tjwlm/* (accessed: 14 September 2007).

Johnny Mnemonic (1995) Film, directed by Robert Longo. Canada/USA: Alliance Communications.

LinkedIn (2003) Website; available at: *www.linkedin.com* (accessed: 20 October 2007).

Loose Change 2nd Edition (2006) Film, directed by Dylan Avery. USA: Louder Than Words.

The Matrix (1999) Film, directed by Andy Warchowski and Larry Warchowski. Australia/USA: Groucho II Film Partnership.

The Matrix Reloaded (2003) Film, directed by Andy Warchowski and Larry Warchowski. USA: Warner Bros Pictures.

The Matrix Revolutions (2003) Film, directed by Andy Warchowski and Larry Warchowski. USA: Warner Bros Pictures.

Minority Report (2002) Film, directed by Stephen Spielberg. USA: Cruise/Wagner Productions.

MySpace (2003) Website; available at: *www.myspace.com* (accessed: 20 October 2007).

Myst (1993) Role-playing game, created by Robyn Miller and Rand Miller. USA: Cyan Worlds.

The Net (1985) Film, directed by Irwin Winkler. USA: Columbia Pictures.

Red Dwarf (1988–1999) Television series. UK: BBC.

Screamers (1995) Film, directed by Christian Duguay. Canada: Allegro Films.

Second Life (2003) Role-playing game, created by Linden Research. USA: Linden Research.

Seksmisja (1984) Film, directed by Juliusz Machulskic. Poland: Zespól Filmowy 'Kadr'.

Shakespeare in Love (1998) Film, directed by John Madden. USA/UK: Bedford Falls Productions.

The Six Million Dollar Man (1974–1978) Television series. USA: Harve Bennett Productions.

Soylent Green (1973) Film, directed by Richard Fleischer. USA: MGM.

Star Trek (1966–1969) Television series. USA: Desilu Productions.

Star Trek: The Next Generation (1987–1994) Television series. USA: Paramount Television.

Star Wars (1977) Film, directed by George Lucas. USA: Lucasfilm.

Star Wars Episode V: The Empire Strikes Back (1980) Film, directed by Irvin Kershner. USA: Lucasfilm

Star Wars Episode VI: The Return of the Jedi (1983) Film, directed by Richard Marquand. USA: Lucasfilm.

Steiner, Peter (1993) 'On the internet no one knows you're a dog', monochrome cartoon, *New Yorker Magazine*, 69(20): 61.

The Terminator (1985) Film, directed by James Cameron. UK/USA: Hemdale Film.

Terminator 2: Judgement Day (1991) Film, directed by James Cameron. France/USA: Canal+.

Terminator 3: Rise of the Machines (2003) Film, directed by Jonathan Mostow. USA/Germany/UK: C-2 Pictures.

Total Recall (1990) Film, directed by Paul Verhoeven. USA: Carolco International.

Tron (1982) Film, directed by Steven Lisberger. USA/Taiwan: Lisberger/Kushner.

Trooper Clerks (1998) Short film, directed by Kevin Smith; available at: *www.trooperclerks.com/films_cartoons.html* (accessed: 14 October 2007).

YouTube (2005) Website; available at: *wwwyoutube.com* (accessed: 20 October 2007).

Vanilla Sky (2001) Film, directed by Cameron Crowe. USA: Artisan Entertainment.

WarGames (1983) Film, directed by John Badham. USA: MGM.

What an Amazing Line-Up (2006) Television advertisement, created by Brendan Wilkins and Rodney Kavanagh. UK: DFGW.

World of Warcraft (1994) Role-playing game, created by Blizzard Entertainment. USA: Vivendi Games.

Index

Printed and bound by CPI Group (UK) Ltd, Croydon, CR0 4YY
03/10/2024
01040437-0009